Nicholas Whitehead is a longtime student of the Western Mystery Traditions, with special interests in Esoteric Christianity and in the practical methods of meditation, ceremony, and inner pilgrimage.

As an early member of the England-based Gareth Knight group and the famed 'Company of Hawkwood,' and as director of studies for a North American based school of the Mysteries, he has spent many years instructing initiates and organizing working groups in both Canada and the USA.

In addition to his esoteric background, he was academically trained in Religious Studies, Philosophy and Classics, and reads several languages. He lectures and directs workshops on many aspects of the Western Mystery Tradition and is the author of several books and articles.

Forthcoming by Nicholas Whitehead:
An Introduction to the Christian Qabalah
The Magi and the Grail

patterns in
Magical
Christianity

nicholas whitehead

SUNCHALICE
BOOKS
1996

Published by

SUN CHALICE BOOKS

PO Box 9703

Albuquerque, New Mexico

USA 87119

Publisher's Cataloging-in-publication Data

Whitehead, Nicholas

    Patterns in Magical Christianity / Nicholas Whitehead

    p.   cm.

    Includes bibliographical references and index

    1. Occultism—Religious Aspects—Christianity

2. Ritual 3. Spiritual life 4. Magic   I. Title

BR115.O3W 1996   248

ISBN 0-9650839-7-7

*Para Marina,
quien es
verdaderamente
un espíritu de luz.*

contents

acknowledgments

I would like to express my gratitude to Lt. Col. Bill Simpson for many hours spent discussing various aspects of this book over its long gestation period, and for his editorial work and useful suggestions in the later stages of the manuscript's preparation.

Equal thanks are due to Mrs. Helga Simpson, for her unflagging support and enthusiasm, and for providing opportunities to present some of the material in a formal public setting.

Thanks are also owed to Mr. Basil Wilby for reading portions of the manuscript and for his valuable remarks; to Mr. Rab Wilkie and Mr. Charles Saad who, each in their own way, have given enthusiastic and insightful support; and to Mr. Bernard Buedden for the loan of important research material.

In addition to most of those listed above, Miss Ana Romero, Miss Eumaira Quintero, and Mr. Felipe Romero deserve thanks for participating in various phases of the testing of the practical exercises.

Finally I would like to express my deepest gratitude to my wife Marina, truly a bright spirit upon this earth, without whose love and support this book could not have been written.

preface

The impetus for this book goes back to 1978 when I embarked upon a course, run by Gareth Knight, in Christian Qabalistic Magic. The course required building a series of symbolic images in the imagination. Several of these impressed me deeply at the time, for they seemed to carry some extraordinary power of regeneration.

Some years later, I rediscovered through conventional academic channels the notion that there are primordial "forms" or archetypes common to, and at the root of, many religious, spiritual, and esoteric philosophies and practices worldwide. I was particularly intrigued by the fact that some of these forms manifested through symbols and patterns strikingly similar to the ones I had encountered in those early days of training.

This in turn sparked my subsequent research into the subject of this book—the role of certain archetypal patterns in Magical Christianity. A large portion of this research involved actual practical experience, by myself and others, employing specialized methods of ritual and inner vision.

I have attempted to combine the insights gained from this practical work with sound esoteric analyses of appropriate background material—traditions, texts, legends, myths, and symbols. The result has been the development of a formal course of training in Magical Christianity, for which this book serves as an initial text. Individuals interested in further details regarding the course are encouraged to write to me through the publisher.

Feast of the Magi, Angel Fire, New Mexico.

introduction

hristianity is a magical religion. This is not so controversial a statement as some might think. For all religious traditions are potentially magical by the simple fact that they embody or employ symbols, myths, and rites that are mediatory, that intend or enable the translation of spiritual energies between levels of reality.

The term "magical," then, refers to a power inherent in the structure of spiritual tradition—the power of *mediation*. And mediation by its very nature always involves or brings about some form of *transformation*. When we speak, therefore, of Magical Christianity, we mean Christianity approached or practiced as a means of bringing about transformation. On one level this refers to a means of mystical transfiguration occurring through developments in the relationship between individual consciousness and Divine Being—between the soul and God. On another level, it refers to active and willing cooperation with the inner orders of beings under the Christ in the transformation, redemption or "Christification" of the cosmos.

As we have suggested, all this is inherent in the symbolic content or magical lore of the tradition itself. It will be useful, therefore, to begin our study by looking at the structure and import of magical symbols.

There are basically two types of magical symbols. There are *inner* or *imaginal symbols* which are symbols built up or received through the inner senses, and *outer* or *material symbols* which are symbols (occurring either by design or in nature) that are experienced with the outer senses.†

It is possible for either an imaginal or a material symbol to become a vehicle for the direct expression of spiritual energy. It is usual, however, for the two types to appear in tandem. A material symbol will often have an imaginal counterpart and *vice versa*. Due to the more fluid structure of imaginal symbols, however, there is a tendency for these to take a superior role, acting as medians or transformers between the physical symbols and archetypal energy.

When this is the case, a practical situation arises that is analogous to a kind of three stage "cone of power." This could be visualized as an inverted cone or funnel with the upper, widest part of the cone originating in the realm of archetypal essence, a lower and narrower section of the cone marking the condensation of archetypal power in an imaginal form, and the tip of the cone being the symbol or point of manifestation on the terrestrial plane.

Another useful analogy could be made with the stained glass windows of a church or cathedral. The pure light of the sun (archetypal essence or energy) passes through a translucent image (the imaginal symbol) which transforms the light (physical symbol) in such a way that it affects, in a specified manner, the physical environment and the consciousness of those who are in that environment.

The latter analogy is quite precise, and is capable of considerable development. The position of the sun during the day and year, for instance, alters the luminosity of the window, and hence the direction of light and emphasis of certain colors within the building. Other factors worthy of meditation would be the play of light and darkness within the cathedral, or the fact that the light goes in from without during the day, yet out from within (assuming candles or other lights are present) during the night.

Bearing in mind the implications of the formula of the "cone

---

†Ultimately, all of the cosmos, inward and outward, is potentially symbolic. It is a matter of discovering or learning to read what the ancients called "the book of nature" that is at issue.

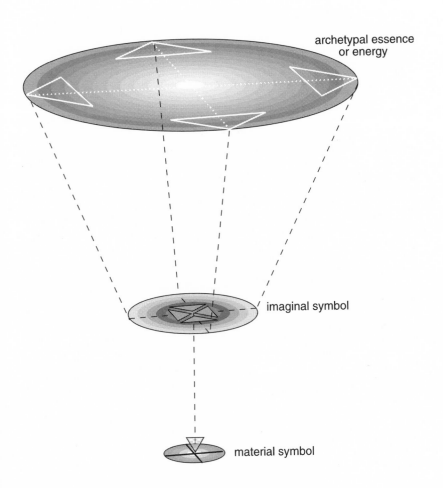

archetypal essence
or energy

imaginal symbol

material symbol

THE CONE OF POWER

of power" and also the two basic types of symbol, we make the following statements about magical symbols in general:

1. Magical symbols are inherently appropriate.
2. Magical symbols always participate in a greater reality.
3. Magical symbols enable the translation of energies between levels of reality.
4. Magical symbols are trans-rational.
5. Magical symbols are polyvalent.
6. Magical symbols tend to assemble in groups expressiing "fields of energy."

Let us remark on these observations one by one.

1. Magical symbols are inherently appropriate.

This simply means that a magical symbol is neither arbitrarily derived, nor the result of mere convention, for its innate form adequately expresses its meanings. Consider the image of a plant. Its roots are in the earth, its flower in the air, within its stem the life bearing sap rises and falls. Because of its intrinsic structure, the plant is a symbol for the ideal spiritual life or growth of the human being. We live upon the earth, with our roots within the land. We are nurtured by the soil on which we live. Yet, without losing our connection with it, it is our destiny to rise above the land, to flower in the crowning glory of the light. This comes about as a combination of our own directed efforts—analogous to the growth of the stem and to the flow of water and sap within it— and the activity of the Light of Divine Grace. For it is in response to the Light that the flower of the spirit develops and unfolds.†

Again note that we can not *make* the plant into a symbol. It simply *is* a magical symbol by virtue of its inherent structure and its role in the rhythmic life of the cosmos.

†It is not for nothing that Christ appears as the Gardener to Mary Magdelene *(John 20:15)*, nor is it without import that he is called "the True Vine" and "the Tree of Life." And there is profound significance in the use of the word "neophyte" (literally, "new plant") to describe one newly entered in the Mysteries.

2. Magical Symbols participate in a greater reality.

Magical symbols always participate in a reality greater than themselves. This property of symbols enables us to gain access to other levels of reality. Such might entail, for instance, an expansion of awareness on a "horizontal" plane—an experience of the inner aspects of nature, other worlds or dimensions and the energies which are to be found there. A similar expansion might also occur on a vertical plane, with symbols acting as transformers for higher spiritual, or archetypal essences.

Taking again the image of a plant, it is not difficult to see how it participates in something greater than itself, that is, the cosmic cycles of the day and the seasons. As a magical symbol, the plant embodies the movement and rhythms of the life-force within the universe. It therefore posits a bridge to analogous cycles and energies within human life and consciousness. The yearly cycle of vegetation resonates with the life cycle of the human being, not only physically, but psychically and spiritually. It is in fact a well known magical practice to align oneself to the rhythms of the sun, the moon, the seasons, and stars. In so doing, one attempts to align oneself to the circuit of life-force within the cosmos, to become at one with nature in all its visible and invisible aspects.

On the other hand, the growth direction of a plant is vertical. This vertical or axial "destiny" is directly analogous to the spiritual destiny of humankind. Just as a plant is destined to rise between earth and sky, depending upon the influence of both for its existence, so does human consciousness stand as mediator between the elemental world and the realm of pure spirit. Ultimately, having aligned ourselves with Divine Will, it is our spiritual destiny to become participants in the restoration of a broken world, even to become co-redemptors, with Christ, of all creation.

3. Magical symbols enable the translation of energies between levels of reality.

Another thing we can say about magical symbols is that they always involve the translation of energies between one level of reality and another. Magical symbols are by nature the agencies of mediation. Among other things, magical technique involves interacting with symbols using the inner senses: the inner vision, sense of touch, taste, hearing, smell. The inner senses have a natural connection with the outer, physical senses (in fact, they are the same senses "inturned") and hence with the physical body as a whole, the instrument of our outer experience. What this means, is that every use of the inner senses by a trained adept, every time one participates in a magical symbol on inner levels, every time one contacts energy inwardly, there inevitably occurs a translation of this energy to the outer world.

It is a misunderstanding and misuse of this principle of mediation which has given rise to the spate of books and courses which teach one how to obtain personal and financial success through techniques of visualization, "positive thinking," and so on. And it is a dim intuition of this same process which has yielded the endless platitudes and semi-techniques which revolve around the New Age maxim: " You create your own reality."

Rightly understood and applied, however, the principle of mediation transforms one's daily experience, sanctifies it with meaning. A great portion of one's life becomes a kind of spiritual exercise. This does not mean that one's experiences are necessarily any different outwardly than anybody else's. It is that they tend towards a holism, a totality, full-lived in spiritual significance.

4. Magical symbols are trans-rational.

The fourth observation we are going to make about the nature and function of magical symbols is that they are trans-rational. On one level this simply means the significance of magical symbols cannot be grasped by purely intellectual means. They must be experienced, actually participated in, if they are to be understood.

A simple analogy could be found in imagining you had been given the task of helping a blind person who had suddenly gained sight to cope with and understand the experience of seeing color. Could you do this by reciting the scientific theories of optics or the refraction of light, or by describing the principle of a spectrum to this person? Would it not be far more effective if you were to proceed, for instance, by describing green as the color of grass, by having this person touch grass first, then identify its color as green? In other words, the path of the intellectual processes can yield very different results from that of actual experience. To know the theories or explanations of color or of magical symbols is a far cry from the experience of color or symbols.

The trans-rational property of symbols involves matters ranging beyond a mere consideration of the limitations of the intellectual function. It is important we realize that we are talking about a mode of apprehension and understanding which takes place on an entirely different level of awareness. For symbols often present paradoxical experiences or experiences of reality which are capable of being apprehended only *through symbols*. Two examples of this will suffice.

There is an esoteric tradition which states that the way to the stars is through the center of the earth. Now this statement is not logical, at least not in any merely intellectual or rational sense. Yet magical tradition holds that this is no meaningless conundrum but a paradox of profound significance—a significance which can only be grasped through symbols. True, on one level it does serve to convey an important magical principle. Namely that the deepest levels of reality are also the highest. But unless this is something which has been actually experienced, we are guilty of merely replacing one paradox with another. The only way to truly apprehend the meaning of this tradition would be to approach it from an entirely different level than that of the discursive, rational mind.

Let us describe the kind of inner scenario which might be used to experience the significance of this tradition. We might, for example, visualize ourselves in a cavern deep within the heart of the earth. Looking down we see that there is a small hole in the floor. Through this hole we see innumerable stars spread throughout the reaches of space. By meditating on this vision, by feeling ourselves in the cave, looking at the stars, it is possible to experience certain inner aspects of reality which cannot be apprehended through the reasoning processes. These may relate to the relationship between crystals and stars, to various levels of being or of the cosmos, or to something else entirely.

The structure of this exercise itself provides the means by which we could apprehend, more or less directly, the reality behind the paradox.

Our second example is an anecdote or legend related about one Alanus ab Insula or Alan Lille. Alanus is regarded as one of the really great poets of the Middle Ages, and he was known as *doctor universalis*, a master teacher who was conversant in all the known fields of learning of his time.

Alanus lived and taught in Paris in the latter part of the twelfth century. According to tradition, one evening he was walking along the Seine River mulling over the subject of his lecture to be given the next morning. He was to talk on the nature of Divine Being. As he walked along thinking of an appropriate approach to his subject, he noticed a young boy playing in the sand near the edge of the river.

The little boy had dug a small hole in the sand and he was happily filling it with water which he carried over from the river in a wooden spoon. Alanus stopped and, having mentioned who he was and what he was about, stood watching the boy's play for a while.

Intrigued by the strange activity, Alanus finally asked him what he was doing. The boy replied that he was going to pour all the water of the river into the hole he had dug. With a patronizing smile, Alanus remarked that this would be quite impossible. One could not possibly pour all the water of the river into that little hole! The boy seemed thoughtful for a moment, then looking the great doctor full in the face, replied that it would be equally impossible for Alanus to speak about the nature of God!

Alanus was totally shattered. Reeling from the immensity of the truth spoken by the child, he staggered off home without a further word. The next day he showed up at the lecture hall as expected. But instead of beginning his lesson, he turned to the students, tore his outer robe from his body and walked out, never to return. It is said that he eventually entered a monastery and there carried out the duties of a shepherd.

We can see how this story illustrates that symbols operate beyond the level of mere discursive reasoning. The image of the child trying to pour the Seine into a little hole conveys far more about the Mystery of God, of Universal Being, about the relationship between Ultimate Being and human consciousness, than volumes of learned intellectual postulations possibly could. We see how a symbol can convey in a split second so profound a revelation that it really transforms one's outlook.

5. Magical symbols are polyvalent.

The fifth statement we shall make about magical symbols is that they are polyvalent. The term comes from "poly" meaning "many," and "valens" which translates as "value," "worth," or "meaning." In other words, a symbol cannot be fully understood by any single meaning, or on any one level of experience. A symbol always participates in a spectrum of significance, an entire range of meaning.

The characteristic which symbols have of simultaneously revealing a broad range of significance means that symbols often participate in more than one "system" or archetypal pattern at the same time. Take, for instance, the image of fire. As a symbol of the Power of God, fire manifests both Divine Justice and Divine Illumination (it can blast as well as bless)—two essentially opposite meanings. But fire will also be found expressing many nuances of meaning between these two extremes: as a symbol of the Divine presence (as in the burning bush, for instance), or of the warm, nurturing womb, the Blessed Heart, or Cosmic Center (as in the hearth fire), or again as a symbol of wisdom, knowledge, passion or purification. Magical symbols are thus not so much like two-edged swords as like multifaceted jewels or many-branched trees.

In practical terms this quality enables one to experience a wide range of related inner energies simultaneously. To some degree also, the polyvalence of symbols accounts for the apparent differences in reaction among a group of people to a given meditation or other form of magical or mystical working. There is a kind of "natural selection" operative in the structure of magical symbols by which, for any of a large number of reasons, various levels of conscious inner experience may be closed to one person yet open to another.

6. Symbolic fields: magical glyphs and magical patterns.

In actual experience magical symbols rarely appear as single isolated images. They are often grouped together in significant ways. Most magical workings make use of a certain range of symbolism, a certain group of meaningfully interrelated images and actions. We call such groups "symbolic fields" because the symbols used in any magical operation constitute a unique array of inner energies, an inner energy field, which has a specific effect on consciousness and matter. This is not to imply that there are rigid rules or recipes which can be mechanically applied so as to yield a desired effect. The practical development of a symbolic field (as in a magical journey or ritual) is rather like the creation of a painting, poem or other work of art—the product of a balanced mix of technical expertise, intuitive perception, and inspired activity.

There are two main types of symbolic field. There is the *magical glyph*, which consists of a particular dominant or central image together with a set of sub-symbols that cohere through their shared resonance or "vibration" with the dominant image. Examples of magical glyphs might be found in any of the Tarot images, for instance, where a central figure is given certain accouterments, is associated with a symbolic landscape, stands in a certain pose, etc.,. Other examples are to be found in the icons and statuary of shrines and temples, the structure of myth and legend and of certain forms of inner journey.

The second class of symbolic field is known as the *magical pattern*. Magical patterns are of a nature more complex than magical glyphs, and indeed are often composed of a set of glyphs arranged according to some archetypal pattern of relationships (usually in the form of numerical or geometric configurations). They might well, in fact, be termed "master glyphs." Examples are: the Qabalistic Tree of Life, the sequence of the Tarot Trumps, certain temples, churches and cathedrals, the magic wheel or circle, and the zodiac. Indeed, the inherent character of this latter, the great round of the zodiac, provides a useful analogy for understanding the relationship between magical patterns, magical glyphs, and magical symbols. The individual stars are like magical symbols, the constellations are glyphs and the zodiac as a whole is a magical pattern. Meditation upon this analogy will be repaid with insight.

All theoretical knowledge regarding the complex structure and function of magical symbols is pointless unless given practical expression. In the Christian Mysteries such practical work is based upon the techniques of magic. Magic, as we have already suggested, is a means of bringing about transformation (some would say, "transformation in consciousness") through the power of mediation. A magician is above all a mediator. A Christian magician is a mediator who works under the aegis of the Christ, and who in companionship with others—masters, saints, angels, magi, etc.—works to bring about the restoration or redemption of the world in both its inner and outer aspects. Christian Magic is therefore a specialized form of spiritual service to God and one's fellow creatures.

Many people are shocked by the use of the term "Christian Magic." But, in spite of the gross misunderstandings and negative press associated with the word "magic," it really is the most accurate term to describe this form of religious activity.

Christian Magic is universal in scope. Its practitioners, in accordance with the belief that Christ came not to condemn the old but to fulfill it, work in many magical traditions, within many cycles of legend and mythology.† These function as doorways to the inner side of creation, portals to unseen energies and entities. Such matters are not undertaken with any sense of missionary zeal. Nor should there be unbalanced attempts at "converting" others (whether they be resident on the outer or the inner planes). Rather, the Christian mage works in an attitude of selfless Compassion, bringing healing and balance to little suspected areas of creation.

Because of this inherent ecumenical spirit, what we have called "Magical Christianity" is really but one area of experience within the general field of the Christian Mysteries. It is, however, the most important area of experience, being embedded in the foundational or root tradition. Magical Christianity is not a new religion, it is not even a new aspect of an old reli-

---

†Augustine of Hippo: "The very thing that is now called the Christian religion was not wanting amongst the ancients from the beginning of the human race, until Christ came in the flesh, after which the true religion, which already existed, began to be called "Christian." *(Retr. I:13:3)*

gion. It is a specialized aspect of religious life, which has been present within the Christian tradition from the start. It may not have been always clearly visible, or readily identifiable or accessible, but it has always been present. And so it will continue, *mutatis mutandis,* as long as there are dedicated souls willing and able to take up the spark of inspiration, fan it into flame, and pass on the torch to others.

The purpose of this book is to set forth certain aspects of the magical lore of Christianity. It has also been our intent to give out a series of practical exercises that will provide a cornerstone of inner experience for those who seek initiation into the deep and profound way of transformation and spiritual service that is the Christian Mysteries:

Ex Deo nascimur,

In Jesu morimur,

Per Spiritum Sanctum reviviscimus.

There is a blessing upon all who serve.

AUTHOR'S NOTE:

The exercises presented in this book have been carefully graded and tested, and are configured so as to enable the aspirant to experience the three primary methods of Christian Magic: *meditation, pathworking* or *inner pilgrimage,* and *ritual.* These, it must be added, will not yield of their fruits unless approached in an attitude of *contemplation,* that is, unless undertaken in a sense of loving service to Divine Being.

A period of approximately two to three weeks, preferably twice a day for at least ten minutes each time, is recommended for the performance of the practical work. Each exercise ends with the proposal that one recite an appropriate word or phrase which encapsulates the energies experienced in that exercise. With a little practice, this should enable you to contact the relevant inner powers by simply reciting your sequence of ritual words or phrases. The sequence as a whole thus becomes a kind of magical rosary or litany. Indeed, the suggested phrases appearing at the end of the exercises for the first six chapters are incoporated into the litany that forms the concluding practical work for the book.

Professional recordings giving expanded versions of the exercises with appropriate sound effects and music are also available from the publisher.

The complete set of four double-sided cassette tapes containing all eight exercises may be obtained by sending $12.95 (includes postage) to :

SUN CHALICE BOOKS
PO Box 9703
Albuquerque, New Mexico
USA 87119

PATTERNS IN MAGICAL CHRISTIANITY

Í

the
sphere

In the beginning God created the heaven and the earth. And the earth was without form, and void; and darkness was upon the face of the deep. And the Spirit of God moved upon the face of the waters *(Genesis 1:1-1:3).*

In his commentary on this passage, James of Edessa (ca. 535) remarks that the earth was originally formless because it was surrounded by the primordial sea "like the embryo is surrounded by the membranes in its mother's womb." He goes on:

> Now God rent this primordial sea. Then he ordered the earth to give up its character of a smooth globe; and he made protuberances and holes, heights and depths on its surface so that the waters were gathered and taken from its surface and the earth could appear.[109]

Two aspects of James' exegesis interest us in particular. One, he draws an analogy between the proto-earth and an embryo, thus evoking the image of a cosmic womb. And two, the earth was originally a perfect sphere. As we shall see, the images of cosmic womb, and globe hold special initiatory importance, for they symbolize at one and the same time primordial wholeness, latent potentiality, and realized perfection.

An image closely related to the cosmic womb and sphere is the cosmic egg.† It is worth commenting that in Hebrew the word for the moving of the Spirit of God over the waters (*rahaf*), means not only "moving," but "brooding" or "hatching," suggesting that the Genesis myth was, indeed, at one time expressed through the image of a cosmogonic egg. Moreover, the text of *Genesis 1* where God separates the upper and lower waters by creating the firmament easily evokes the image of a cosmic dome or sphere.

As far as Christianity is concerned, the myth of *Genesis* has always provided the general pattern for the cosmogonic sequence. However, this pattern was sharpened, defined, and focused through influences best characterized as "Orphic." The impact of the Orphic traditions on the pictorial representations of Christ in the catacombs is well known. Less well known is the influence of Orphism on early Christian perceptions regarding the structure and symbolic "shape" of the cosmos.

According to Orphic myth, in the beginning was chaos, being neither light nor darkness, neither dry nor moist, neither hot nor cold, all was formless, unbounded, undifferentiated substance. Yet chaos itself was eventually contained or bound in the shape of a great egg. The egg divided and the primal, androgynous being—Phanes, the Shining One—was born. At that moment the Three Worlds and the Four Elements came into being. The upper hemisphere of the cosmic egg became the dome of the heavens, while the lower hemisphere became the bowl of the underworld and the foundation for the terrestrial world.

Disregarding for the moment the figure of Phanes, we observe that the imagery presented above is generally consonant with the Old Testament traditions which, as we have said, were the source *sine qua non* for early Christian conceptions about the genesis and structure of the cosmos. Not only do we have a common image of creation through separation, but the doctrine of three worlds or cosmic regions was known to nearly

†As with all Primordial Symbols, the cosmic egg and/or sphere is found in sacred contexts (myths, rituals, legends, songs, etc.,) throughout the world. One finds the image in areas as diverse and far-flung as Polynesia, Indonesia, Estonia, Latvia, Finland, Persia, Peru, Central America, West Africa, Egypt, Japan, China, Tibet, India, Arabia, and others.[48]

all ancient cultures, and forms part of the cosmological model that runs through both Old and New Testaments.

During the long course of Christian tradition and visionary experience, we are not surprised to find the cosmic images of egg and sphere cropping up often, sometimes closely and consciously associated with each other.† The *Recognitions* and *Homilies* ascribed to Clement of Rome (ca. 99 A.D.), both recount the Orphic cosmogony using the terms for "egg" and "globe" interchangeably.[1] In his work *de Imagine Mundi*, Honorius of Auton (ca. 1125) writes that the spherical universe resembles an egg, not only in shape, but in content. Different cosmic zones are reflected in the shell, albumen, and yoke of the egg, for instance.[78] In her earlier visions, as recorded in the *Skivias*,[80] Hildegard of Bingen (1100-1181) saw the cosmos in the shape of an egg, while in her later visions the image of a sphere occurs.

The sphere figures in the works of other great mystics and thinkers too. Julian of Norwich (ca. 1423), in her *Showings*, relates how during one of her visionary experiences she became aware of a small object "as round as any ball" resting in her hand. "What is it?" she asked. And the answer came: "It is everything which is made."[56] The great *doctor universalis*, Alan of Lille (d. 1203), drawing on little known hermetic traditions, wrote a treatise on the "intelligible sphere whose center is everywhere and whose circumference is nowhere."[19]

Taken purely in terms of its geometry, the sphere is the symbol of wholeness and primal totality *par excellence*. Its significance as a symbol of perfect balance is rendered by its "isotropic" nature.

---

†The recurrence in the Christian Tradition of these two images, either singly or together, was undoubtedly aided and abetted by the influence of the Neoplatonist philosophers whose powerful impact on Christian mystical philosophy and metaphysics is undisputed: "Let us then form a mental image of this cosmos .... so that whatever ... comes first into the mind as the 'one' (as for instance, the outermost sphere of the fixed stars), there immediately follows also the sight of the semblance of the sun, and together with it that of the other stars or planetary spheres, and the earth and sea, and all things living, as though in one transparent sphere.... Let there then be in the soul some semblance of a sphere of light, having all things in it.... Then invoking God who has made the reality of which you hold the phantom in your consciousness, pray that He may come" Plotinus (ca. A. D. 250).[69] And according to Macrobius (ca.. A. D. 410*)*, the egg was greatly revered in the mysteries "because of its oval, almost spherical, shape which has no opening of any kind, and because it contains life in itself."[12]

Man, the microcosm in the sphere of the cosmos. From an illustrated codex of St. Hildegard of Bingen.

That is, it possesses the same properties in all directions. In a sense, the sphere contains within itself all other figures,† for, given equal surface area, a sphere has greater volume than any other shape.‡

At this level, the sphere signifies undifferentiated possibility. The idea of latent potentiality is further suggested by the fact that a sphere has no determined axis. It is when a sphere is defined by an axis that it can be said to represent the manifestation or actualization of possibility. Creation takes place, therefore, when the primordial sphere or cosmogonic egg is fixed along an axis.

The Cosmic Axis takes many forms in the various traditions: a sacred pole or tree (e.g. the Cross, the Tree of Life), a sword, spear, pillar, tower, or mountain, or, as in the Orphic Mysteries and in Esoteric Christian circles, a divine being. Sometimes, in myth and symbol, the presence of the Axis is

---

†"Now for that Living Creature which is designed to embrace within itself all living creatures the fitting shape will be that which comprises within itself all the shapes there are; wherefore He wrought it into a round, in the shape of a sphere. . . " Plato, *Timaeus, 33.*

‡This is easier to visualize in two dimensional terms. For example, the area of a circle of a given circumference is greater than the area of, say, a square with the same perimeter.

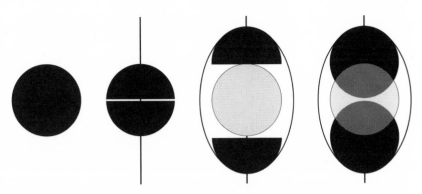

The sphere, the egg, and the Three Worlds.

more subtly disclosed through images like the separation of the two halves of the cosmogonic egg, or the elongation of the primordial sphere.

Both these symbolic movements-separation and elongation-yield, it need hardly be said, an ovoid configuration. This more typical egg-like shape relates, in a very practical, esoteric sense, to the aforementioned pattern of three inter-penetrating worlds or cosmic zones.†

It will be noted again that the image of the cosmic womb also partakes of the sphere's sacred geometry (through the roundness of pregnancy) just as, especially in relation to the mysteries of creation, birth, and rebirth, it shares in the symbolism of the cosmic egg. Up to a point, then, these three images-the sphere, the womb, the egg-are interchangeable. During certain ceremonies, for instance, both the Pueblo and the Pawnee Indians employ two bowls, one inverted over the other, to represent the spherical cosmos.[82] For the Pueblo, at least, this image is also linked to the concept of the cosmic womb. Among the Pueblo too, the connection extends to sacred architecture. The ceremonial lodges, known as *kivas,* are round semi-subterranean structures obviously based upon the pattern of an earth womb.

A similar pattern is probably the basis for the thousands of prehistoric mound burials found by European settlers along

†For a more detailed consideration of the Three Worlds see below Chaps. vi-vii.

Neolithic burial mound. Holland.

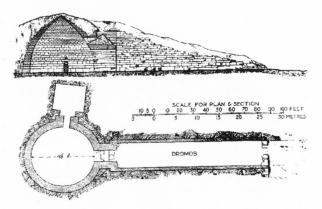

This *tholos* or "beehive" tomb at Mycenae, Greece combines the motifs of cosmic dome and sacred cave (cosmic womb) circa 1185 B.C.

Great Stupa at Sanchi, Central India.

Indian mound. Ohio, U.S.A.

the river valleys of eastern North America. The bodies were sometimes placed in a flexed, fetal position as if being returned to the cosmic womb that they may be ready for rebirth. In fact, the Choctaw Indians referred to the larger mounds as "navels."[91] †

These patterns of sphericity and of birth and rebirth, no matter what mythic image or combination of images may have originally articulated them, lie at the root of similar burial structures known from earliest times in Europe, Asia, and the Middle East. We need only cite the numerous burial mounds of the Neolithic period in Europe; the *tholoi* or "beehive" tombs which are found all over the ancient Mediterranean world; the reliquary stupas distributed throughout the Buddhist world; the round tombs of North Africa; the rock-cut domical tombs which occur widely in the Middle East; not to mention the adoption and use of these forms throughout the Roman Empire. Moreover, the widespread occurrence in the Hellenistic period of these types of structures provided a ready store of architectural symbolism for the early Christian masons and builders.

†This also suggests their importance as nodes of power in the landscape (see below Chapter iv.

Chamber in the catacomb of Calixtus. Note the development of three characteristic elements of catacomb construction: the *arcosolium*, the *cubiculum*, and the *luminaria*—A round, vaulted ceiling is set upon a square base with illumination provided by a light well. These three elements prefigure the structural components—square base, dome, and oculus—of the first major sacred edifice in Christianity, the Holy Sepulcher in

The earliest extant Christian burials, those in the catacombs, are associated with the egg and the sphere through the dome and arch forms which appear in connection with them, and also through the presence of eggshells in some of the graves. They are likewise connected to the symbolism of the cosmic womb through the caves themselves. The cavern has long been treated in sacred lore as the womb of the Earth Mother. It is of interest to note that there is beneath the Church of the Nativity at Bethlehem a sacred cave where, according to a well-known tradition of great antiquity, Christ was born of the Virgin Mother.

At any rate, the cosmic symbolism and function of these underground complexes was transferred above ground and merged with the existing Roman and Middle Eastern forms to yield the elaborated symbolic developments incorporated into the first churches. Most early Christian churches were either aisled basilicas or domed martyria. In the latter, a number of the martyrs' graves have been found to contain small marble eggs.

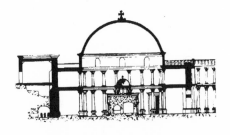

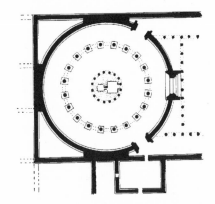

Section and plan of the Holy Sepulcher, Jerusalem- circa 325 A.D.

The martyria were certainly based upon the patterns infused into the architecture of the original Holy Sepulcher in Jerusalem. This church, like all sacred enclosures and edifices, replicated the structure of the cosmos. The upper dome, representing the starry heavens, and accordingly decorated with stars, sat upon a lower rotunda (representing the physical plane) marked with a niche at each of the cardinal directions. At the center of the rotunda was a shrine or edicule leading down to the actual cavern-tomb of Christ representing, as it were, the underworld entrance.

The same symbolism resurfaces, transformed, in the churches of the Romanesque and Gothic periods where it is expressed primarily through the vault, the arch (including the arched portals), the tower, the cruciform nave, the subterranean crypt, and, in a special way, in the Gothic rose windows. The ideal Gothic cathedral has three rose windows representing, among other things, the three cosmic regions. At Chartres,

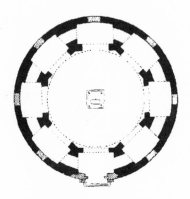

Floor plan of martyrium
at Hieropolis, Syria.

for example, the focus of the northern window is the Christ Child, that is, the Incarnated Logos in the terrestrial world. The western rose—the West is traditionally one of the points of entry to the underworld—depicts Christ in Judgment over the dead. The rose of the South, place of celestial fire and spirit, shows the Ascended Christ in Majesty over the cosmos.

The symbolism underlying the configuration of windows in a Gothic cathedral is complex and profound. We note here, however, that the eastern walls in Gothic cathedrals and churches do not generally sport rose windows. What does commonly appear is a single or connected series of relatively narrow, tall windows suggesting the symbolism of pillar or axis. Even when taken simply in terms of position and shape, these windows reflect two major themes closely linked to the Mystery of Cosmic Redemption: the theme of the rebirth of creation, filtered through the symbolism of the East as the beginning point of the diurnal and seasonal cycles; and the theme of realignment of the three cosmic regions or worlds through the axial power of the "Resurrection Body" of Christ. Indeed, the windows of the East sometimes do depict the Resurrected Christ.

According to ancient Christian tradition, the universe was created at Eastertide† Christ's Resurrection, then, in that it

---

†As witness, the medieval practice of reciting the Creation Text of *Genesis I* during the Easter Vigil. Closely related also are certain astrological factors which link Easter and the Creation Myth. The sun, along with the moon in its full phase, was created at the beginning of time, that is, in Aries, the first sign of the Zodiac. Likewise Easter is traditionally dated each year with reference to the first full moon occurring after the sun has entered the sign Aries (the Spring Equinox).

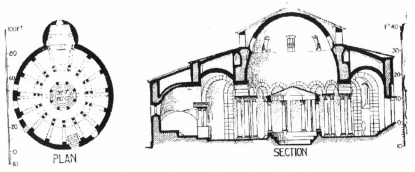

Baptistery at Nocera, Italy - circa 350 A.D.

brought about the birth of a "new creation," reiterates, on a higher octave, the primeval cosmogonic process.† Now this idea of a new creation carries within it the possibility of the spiritual rebirth, that is, the initiation, of the individual soul. It is precisely because the domed, tombed churches embodied the archetypal structures of a redeemed or perfected cosmic order that they became the favored places for the initiation rites. The identification of the baptismal font itself with the bowl or *krater* of the underworld enabled the candidate to ritually enact the Mysteries of Christ's Descent to the Underworld and subsequent Resurrection. This is clearly implied by the following article from the Council of Toledo (633 A.D.): "The immersion in water is as a descent to the underworld, and the coming forth again from the water is a resurrection."[66]

To a large extent, the themes of creation and resurrection underlie the numerous rites and traditions which have accrued to Easter Eggs. One or two examples from the vast treasure-house of traditional lore will suffice to illustrate our point. At Easter Mass, during the Middle Ages, it was customary to have colored eggs near the altar. One of these would be placed in a model "tomb" and then removed by the priests at the appropriate moment. As this was done, the ritual phrase "Christ is risen" would be recited.[84] We might also note William of

---

†"But when a new people was created...,it was no longer necessary for them to observe the end of the first creation, but rather to seek the beginning of the second. And what is this, but the day on which the Lord rose again. It is from here that the new creation began.... God ceased His making of the first creation...; but the second creation has no end."--Athanasius, *de sabbatis*.[21]

Phanes in the egg. Modena, Italy.

Normandy's thirteenth century comparison of the emergence of a chick from an egg to the Resurrected Christ bursting forth from the tomb,[12] and a rather striking image, occurring on a font at Alsleben bei Zerbst in Germany, shows Christ at the Resurrection emerging from an egg.[84]

One recalls in all of this the mythical Phanes who sprang from the Egg of Creation. Phanes, like Adam and numerous other primal ancestors, is androgynous, one in whom the male-female polarities are united, a "total" being. This notion of primordial wholeness underpins a great complex of spiritual traditions and techniques worldwide. In certain Chinese myths, for example, the two sexes were originally embodied in the precosmic "breathing" which eventually formed itself into a great egg. From the egg, the cosmic regions of heaven and earth were then born. This myth has been linked to Taoist meditation techniques said to aid the initiate in achieving "immortality."[33]

The theme of the union of opposites in relation to the "Res-

Detail from an Icon. Christ ascending in a sphere. School of Novgorod, Russia *(16th century)*.

urrection Body" which forms an important aspect of esoteric Christian teaching and practice is too complex and extensive to be taken up in detail at this time. We will content ourselves, therefore, with a few keynote remarks. The coincidence of opposites is implicit, for example, in certain Eastern Orthodox icons representing Christ surrounded by a sphere of light, particularly at the Nativity, Transfiguration, Resurrection and Ascension. We need hardly repeat here the significance of the sphere as a symbol of primordial totality, wholeness, perfection, and so on.

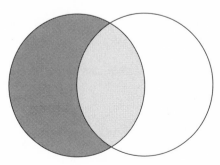

The *vesica piscis*.

A similar iconography occurs in the Western Church, though here the idea of the resolution of opposites is usually represented in the underlying geometry of the mandorla or glory, the almond of light which surrounds the figure of the Resurrected Christ. This shape is most simply gener-

Christ in the mandorla. Chartres Cathedral, France.

ated by the intersection of two circles. The mandorla or *vesica piscis* thus signifies the integral nature of the Resurrected One who, since all opposites are united in him, embodies, as it were, the characteristics of a "third race " in which "there is no male and female"† *(Galatians 3:28)*: "All those will be astonished that see me. For from another race am I," say the *Odes of Solomon (Ode 41)* in reference to the initiatory experience in an early esoteric Christian community. The language is poetic and metaphoric, and at the same time symbolic and practical. We do well to keep in mind, however, that there is little correspondence here with the thin notions of popular psychology or New Age teachings regarding "getting in touch with one's male or female side." The "language of androgyny" is an ancient esoteric convention and refers to the union, balancing, or resolution of all those forces within and without the human soul which tend, otherwise, to a state of polarization or conflict.

---

†Interesting too is that the rendering of the *vesica piscis* or mandorla is related to the "squaring of the circle" which itself lies at the root of certain esoteric Masonic traditions incorporated into the cathedrals of the Middle Ages. In a certain sense, the square (or cube) represents the manifestation or fulfillment of the potentiality inherent in the circle (or sphere) Thus the Sphere of Creation becomes ultimately the foursquare "New Jerusalem," the restoration of the paradisal realm on a new level.

The idea of perfect wholeness contained within the symbolism of egg and sphere also finds expression in the clairvoyant perception of the human aura. The aura is generally described as an ovoid or spherical emanation of light encompassing the human form. According to esoteric teaching, the aura is at once the residue of man's primordial wholeness, and the archetype of restored perfection. It is both a remnant of the "Adamic state" which existed before the human constitution divided into opposites,† and the ultimate pattern of regeneration in Christ who is "the new Adam." It is therefore not surprising that those with developed clairvoyant powers are able to sense or "see" in the aura the physical, psychic, and spiritual health of an individual. This is normally perceived in terms of colors, shades, movements and patterns of light in the aura. These observations are then interpreted by means of their inherent symbolism in ways that describe the various areas of balance and imbalance within the person. It is also possible to effect healing or changes in consciousness by visualizing changes in the hue, position, shape, or fluctuation of the auric light.

All valid esoteric work has a practical, experiential, dimension. And, indeed, underpinning the theoretical content of this chapter (as of all the chapters) are certain principles which can only be fully realized from within the crucible of actual inner experience. Let us therefore practice the following exercise:

Exercise:
THE SPHERE OF CREATION

Use *the Kenotic Opening* (see appendix) to enter the deep peace. Become aware, deep within your being, of a tiny spark of light. This grows into a sphere which expands to encompass you and fill the cosmos.

Visualize the upper half of the cosmic sphere to be

---

†Certain legends speak of Adam as originally having a spherical body.

gold, the lower half to be silver. The sphere now turns indigo blue and you become aware of the shining stars all around you.

A landscape solidifies. You stand upon a plateau at the summit of a mountain. Near you runs a stream, soon becoming a river which empties into a great sea.

The full moon rises from your right and illumines the landscape with its silvery light. It sets to your left. At the point where the moon rose, the sun now rises, glorifying all the world with new light and life. You hear birds singing their dawn chorus. You become aware of a great host of angelic beings all around you and you commune with them. The sun sets and the sphere darkens again.

The sphere contracts, drawing the stars together so that their lights merge and you are at the center of a sphere of pure starlight which coincides with the boundary of your aura. You meditate upon this, repeating to your self as you do so an appropriate ritual phrase (*suggestions*: "A shining sphere of cosmic love;" "Blessed are those who are centered in Love;" "Be hallowed by a sacred sphere.").

íí

the
axís

Many early Christian churches had round apertures, openings to the sky, located at the center of their domes. One can imagine the interior of one of these churches lit by the beam of sunlight that entered the church during the morning hours, and which at midday would shine straight down upon the central altar in a great column of light.

The column of light constitutes, as it were, a Cosmic Axis. The Axis occurs in the guise of many other images in the Christian Tradition, such as, the Tree of Life, the ladder, the mountain, the pillar, the stellar ray, the lance or spear, the staff and the crosier, the bell tower, the spire, and so on. All of these images, moreover, may be subsumed to, and incorporated into, the symbolism of the Cross of Christ and, ultimately, to the very Body of Christ.

It will be well worthwhile to look more closely at some of these symbols as a prelude to our summary of the esoteric significance and spiritual function of the Cosmic Axis. The Tree of Life is a primordial image, almost universally disseminated in both time and space. In its general symbolism it renders an image of the magical structure of the cosmos. The trunk, through which passes the rise and fall of the vital sap, stretches upward through the middle, earthly plane. The roots, drawing nutrients from the deep earth, represent the levels, stages, and grades of descent into the lower underworld realms, just as the branches

Through its close association with Roman civilization, early Christian architecture inherited many aspects of ancient cosmic symbolism. Shown above is a drawing of the Pantheon built by the Roman emperor Hadrian, circa 124 A.D. Note the column of sunlight entering through the *oculus* in the dome.

A *kiva* with axial ladder. In the distance, one of the four sacred mountains that define the boundaries of the Tewa civilization (see Chapter iv). New Mexico, U.S.A.

Inside the *kiva*.

Sacred birds perch atop these cross shaped shaman poles.

yielding leaf and fruit above show the stages of ascent through the heavens. From time immemorial, the cosmic schema reflected in the Tree of Life has provided a means of orientation toward spiritual beings and sacred powers, as well as an itinerary for passage between one cosmic plane or region and another. When the Altaic shaman climbs his seven-notched birch pole, he simultaneously ascends, in vision, the Tree of Life through the celestial planes.[36] A similar symbolism comes into play among the Pueblo Indians of New Mexico whose sacred *kivas* are entered and exited by a ladder which extends through a central hole in the roof. Origen and Celsus mention the use in the Mithraic Mysteries of a ladder of seven rungs of seven different metals. The rungs represent the different heavens through which the initiate ascends in order to attain the Empyrean.[72] In the *Old Testament* we read of Jacob's dream of a ladder reaching from earth to heaven and "the angels of God were ascending and descending on it" *(Gen. 28:10 ff)*.

In the Christian Tradition, the ladder† has a long history. We must emphasize that almost without exception, wherever it occurs, from earliest times right through the Middle Ages, the image of the ladder retains its practical dimension as a means of mystical ascent and descent. Thus it is said that a sixth cen-

†Another important image that developed out of the ladder and which serves a similar function, is the mystic spiral stair.

This *ragulée* cross has seven notches on the
upright representing the seven heavens.

tury Irish bishop, Maedoc of Ferns, one day ascended a golden
ladder reaching from earth to heaven. When he returned his
face shone with a dazzling light.[96] In the twelfth century,
Honorius of Auton describes the mode through which the soul
attains visions of the different heavens and ultimately knowledge of God as a "great heavenly ladder" of ordered, congruent
grades or rungs. A ladder which rises from earth to heaven and
which if ascended in the correct manner leads to the vision of
"the kingdom of glory in all its beauty."[78]

From early times too, Jacob's Ladder was associated with the
Cross. "The Cross... is the ladder of Jacob with angels ascending
and descending upon it, with the Lord standing at the upper-
most rung," writes an anonymous Greek at the beginning of the
third century.[17] Drawing on the same body of traditions, Andrew
of Crete (ca. 625), remarks that "the Cross is a ladder leading to
heaven."[74] According to Theophanes Keramous (ca. 1135), when
"Jacob lay down to sleep upon the stone, there was shown to
him in a vision a ladder which extended from earth through all
the spheres of the heavens.... To the eye of the soul, this ladder
clearly figures the Cross."[76] It is also worth noting that in some
renditions the Cross is shown with seven notches along the upright suggesting, in a remarkable parallel to the notched pole of
the shamans, a sevenfold hierarchy of celestial planes and powers.[33] This septenary pattern of ascensional symbolism has always played an important part in magical Christian practice. In
modern times it is generally incorporated into the tenfold pattern of spheres and energies known as the Qabalistic Tree of

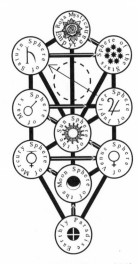

The Cross as the Tree of Life. The sacred pelican nests in the top of the tree. From a Spanish Manuscript.

One version of the Tree of Life as it appears today in Esoteric Traditions. This one indicates a simplified pattern of mystical ascent based upon the imagery of Dante's *Paradiso.*

Life. Rightly understood, this very practical and inherently flexible glyph provides, among much else, a means of orientation towards the beings and forces of the inner creation and a way of approaching the stages of mystical ascent.

Returning to the general symbolism of the Cosmic Tree, let us remark that the Tree not only presents an analog for the threefold structure of the cosmos, but, also embodies the vital processes of periodic renewal and regeneration that pervade the entire creation. This is one reason the Tree is almost universally associated with the idea of spiritual transformation. It is also why in the Christian Tradition the Tree of Life is so closely tied to the symbolism of the Cross and hence to the Redemption of Adam and the Resurrection of Christ.

According to one set of traditions, when Adam was near death, he asked his son Seth to journey to the paradisal realm in order to obtain the fruit of immortality from the Tree of Life. He was able to acquire, however, only three seeds which were given to him by the archangelic guardian of Paradise. These he placed under Adam's tongue. Though Adam died three days later, the seeds sprouted from his grave, yielding three trees growing so close together that they merged into one.† Adam's body was taken aboard the ark by Noah and was eventually buried at Golgotha. After many adventures, including its incorporation into the lintel of the Temple of Solomon,‡ and its use as a rod of healing by David, the wood of the Tree was used to make the Cross of the Crucifixion. And as Christ's side was pierced with the Lance of Longinus, his blood spilt upon Adam's skull and Adam was thus redeemed.[39, 63]

There is a considerable amount of esoteric wisdom to be gleaned from this cycle of legends. What concerns us for the moment, however, is the clear link established between the Tree of Life and the Cross of Christ. For it is only with an awareness of these two as expressions of the Axis that certain elements of the redemptive, healing, and regenerative powers traditionally assigned to the symbol and sign of the Cross in Magical Christianity can be fully understood.

Another line of tradition links the Universal Axis to the Incarnation by tracing the history of a staff made from the wood of the Tree of Life. This staff, bearing the secret name of God upon it, was brought out of the Garden of Eden by Adam from

---

†The three types of tree usually mentioned are the palm, the cypress and the cedar. These three have had their own folklore and symbolism for millennia. The symbolism marks each tree as pertaining to one of the three cosmic regions. The attributions are briefly as follows:

a) The palm is associated with eternity, purity and the Celestial World.

b) The cypress is linked with the rites of death and mourning, and relates to the Underworld.

c) The cedar is as associated particularly with regeneration and cyclic processes. It is thus attributed to the Middle World.

The fusion of the trees reflects the power of the staff over the forces of the Three Worlds, and also the power of the Cross as the instrument of regeneration and redemption of the whole cosmos.

‡The mention of the wood of the Cross as a structural component of the original Temple connects to a stream of esoteric teaching regarding the relationship of the Body of Christ to the sacred edifice. In the legend, the proto-cross which will bear the Body of Christ becomes the door leading to the Divine Presence. The traditions encapsulated here find their way well into the Middle Ages reaching their flowering in the Gothic Period. The form of the Church was based upon both the Mystical Body of Christ and the cosmic Cross which were symbolically fused at the Crucifixion.

This remarkable drawing (above) from a medieval Psalter shows Christ on the World Mountain. One end of his axial cross-staff touches the head of a serpent, while the other pokes through the earthly sphere into the realm of stars and celestial powers. Left is a detail from the drawing.

whom it descended to Enoch, Noah, Shem, Abraham, Jacob, Joseph, eventually reaching Jethro, the Priest of Median. One day, Jethro stuck the staff into the earth and was unable to draw it out again, and "all the strong men in Median came and tried to pull it out, yet none succeeded." It was only Moses who was able to draw forth the staff from the ground, and with it he performed many miracles and feats of magic. The staff was handed down until it reached David. After David it continued to be passed on, but the recipients or heirs were now no longer aware of the power and history of the staff.[41]† At last it reached the hands of Joseph the Carpenter, for whom it suddenly blossomed forth as a sign for all that he was the one chosen to wed the Virgin Mary. The symbol of the blossoming staff touches upon a doctrine of considerable importance in esoteric Christian Tradition, namely, that Christ himself "incarnates" the Cosmic Axis.‡

We note again the appearance of Jacob among those who inherited the holy staff. We have already seen the importance which Jacob's Ladder has as an expression of the World Axis. Indeed, this is emphasized even more when we consider the tradition that after his dream, Jacob set up the stone on which he had laid his head as a pillar shrine to God *(Gen. 28:18)*. Obviously, there is a complex iconography surrounding the figure of Jacob and his relation to the Axis. He was, for instance, the father of

---

†The loss of memory of primordial matters is a notion common to many esoteric traditions. In spiritual terms, human beings are seen as falling away from a primal state of perfection. The idea is at the root of those ritual patterns and practices which themselves reflect or embody temporal and cyclic structures as well as those which are fitted to a "calendar" as in the Calendar of Saints. The practical significance of these cyclical or spiral patterns is that they enable the recreation of a primordial event on a recurring (usually yearly) cycle. One might say that linear time is in this way altered to a sacred pattern. Spiritual forces are enabled to spill into the flow of time, saturating the present with primordial power, in a sense, redeeming time. There are deep and important reasons for the early Christian references to Christ as the *anniculus*, the "One Year Old".

‡This doctrine is rather more fully developed in a cycle of traditional stories about the Magi. *The Chronicle of Zuquin*, for instance, relates how the Magi climb the World mountain every year to look for signs of the coming redeemer. Eventually a star appears and a Divine Child descends in a pillar of light to tell the Magi to go to Bethlehem, As the Magi near the cave where the Redeemer is being born, they see a pillar of light descend to the cave filling it with a light brighter than the sun.

In this medieval carving, the
Archangel Michael is holding
an arrow.

the Twelve Tribes of Israel, which on one level makes him the center of a zodiacal arrangement of territory and lineage. Moreover, the episode where he bows his head over his staff to bestow his blessings upon the sons of Joseph *(Gen. 47:31; Hebrews 11:21)*, was taken by John of Damascus (ca. 650 AD), among others, to prefigure Christ hanging upon the Axial Cross of the cosmos raying out his blessings to the world.[75]

It is undoubtedly this strong connection of Jacob with the Axis, that gave the ancient navigating and surveying device known as "Jacob's Staff" its name. The Jacob's Staff was basically a cross-staff along which the medieval navigator, surveyor, or geomancer would site. According to legend, the *locus* of the famous Salisbury Cathedral was chosen by the flight of an arrow. It has been suggested that the Jacob's Staff, in that it resembles a crossbow, may be behind the legend. According to this interpretation, the unlettered peasants would have mistaken the staff for a crossbow and then assumed the existence of an accompanying arrow. One must bear in mind, however, that the terms "arrow," "dart" and "spear" were commonly used during medieval times to designate forces that are, in the broadest sense of the word, "spiritual." Healing texts like the eleventh century *Lacnunga*,[42] for instance, speak of the elven arrows or darts that bring illness, and Teresa of Avila describes a mystical experience wherein a fiery angel pierces her heart with a spear of love.[104] We note here that the English words "spear," and "spire" are virtually identical, and that the French word *fleche*— "arrow"—also refers to a church spire. In other words, the legend

St. George transfixing the dragon.
From a Russian Icon.

of the siting of Salisbury Cathedral by an arrow may have much to do with the axial energies available in the landscape.

The symbolism of the arrow and spear draws in other images of piercing and transfixing. According to Gregory of Elvira (ca. 350 AD), the magical staff with which Moses struck the rock bringing forth the gushing stream of the Waters of Life is the prototype of the Lance of Longinus which pierced the side of Christ releasing the redemptive blood and water into the world.[20] We here touch again upon a version of the "history" of the sacred wood of the Tree of Life, in this case, closely allied with the Waters of Life which themselves hearken back to the four rivers of Paradise. And again too, the themes of regeneration, and redemption appear. But with regard to the lance and its corollary the sword, we enter an enormously rich area of esoteric Christian symbolism and experience.

Of the many dragon fighting legends in Christian tradition, those of St. George and the Archangel Michael are undoubtedly the most important and the most widely dispersed in lore and iconography. These two may, in fact, be taken to represent two aspects or developments of a single esoteric motif.

The legend of St. George is itself comprised of two main mythic components—the martyrdom and the dragon fight—both of which have important esoteric implications and structures. We are here concerned, though, with George the Dragon Slayer who

St. Michael with cross-lance

according to legend was riding one day in the Cappadocian province of Libya where he came upon Sylene, a city being terrorized by a dragon. The countryside surrounding the city had been all "envenomed" and was now a veritable wasteland. Moreover, the citizens had given to sacrificing maidens to appease the dragon. When George arrived the chosen victim happened to be the King's daughter who "had gone forth dressed as a bride to meet her doom." St. George, however, transfixed the dragon with his lance and overthrew it. Then, using the maiden's garter as a harness, led the beast back to the city. Many of the inhabitants of Sylene were baptized. St. George then killed the dragon with his sword and ordered its body carried out into the surrounding fields in four wagons. And the land became fruitful and rich once again.[5, 10]

Let us consider, first of all, how the presence of the dragon turns the countryside to a wasteland. The dragon, in this case represents a manifestation of, or regression to, a fixed, chaotic state, a mode of existence where all is pure potency, undefined, and merely latent— all is in a perpetual state of winter. The first action required for the healing of the land is the transfixing of the dragon by the axial weapon. In most paintings, statues and icons it is the head of the dragon which is pierced by the sword or lance. We might recall here that according to certain rites of construction in India, at the place where the foundation stone for a building will be laid, the master mason drives a stake into the ground in order that the head of the earth serpent may be firmly fixed. In the legend of St. George we saw that the dragon is dispatched after the baptismal (that is, initiatory) rites take place. Indeed, in early Christian ritual the descent into the water was closely linked to the fight with the dragon, just as the rising forth from the water was associated with the ascent of Jacob's Ladder.[24]

We are dealing then, in the legend of St. George, with an initiatory scenario which affects and functions on both individual human and terrestrial environmental levels. For the land is regenerated by the cutting up and sowing of the dragon's parts in all the quarters of the region—Chaos is transformed into Cosmos, ordered and manifested. The exemplary myth for this sequence is the slaying by God of the primordial dragon whose

The seven-headed dragon representing the old cosmic order,
threatens the "new creation" symbolized by the woman clothed with
sun, moon, and stars. It is she who bears the Divine Child,
representative of the redeemed human race.

body is cut up to form the universe.† The initiatory pattern of
death and rebirth, of descent and ascent, contained in the St.
George legend and enacted on a spiritual plane in the ancient
baptismal rites thus echoes and is founded upon a primordial
creative act of God.

The special relationship between the primal generation of
the cosmos and the spiritual regeneration of the initiate, reflects also a metaphysical tension that exists between a human
being and his surroundings. The redemption of the fourfold elemental structure of the soul has immediate and direct effects

---

†Was it not thou that didst cut Rahab
   in pieces,
that didst pierce the dragon?
Was it not thou that didst dry up the
   Sea,
the waters of the great deep....? *(Isaiah 51:9-10)*

Note also that the myth of the primordial dragon slaying is here linked to the separation
of the Waters of *Genesis 1.*

Some Irish and British hermit-monks lived in round towers
symbolizing the Cosmic Axis.

on the environment in which that soul resides, and *vice versa*.

This is a theme which has parallels in certain Grail legends. In particular, we refer to the tales of the Dolorous Stroke which laid the land to waste until it could be restored by one of purest heart and noble spirit. The Dolorous Stroke was brought about by the misuse of the Lance, that is of the powers of the Axis, and this misuse resulted in the wounding of the "King" and the wasting of his realm. The key to the restoration of the broken realm lay in re-establishing the correct relationship between the Lance and the Grail, which, in the sense we are interested in, means the relationship between the Axis and the Center. In light of what has already been said regarding the role of the serpent's head in the fixing of the earth forces, we note that the Grail itself, in some versions of the legend, appears as a bleeding head. Need we mention here that Christ is called "the Head" by the early Church, or recall the bloody image of the Crown of Thorns?†

---

†Probably the charge laid by the Inquisition that the Knights Templar worshipped a head has its basis in secret Order teachings regarding Christ as the Cosmic Center. This would all tie in with the Holy Sepulcher, Golgotha, and the Head of Adam said to have been buried at the foot of the Cross

Christ the axis and embodiment of the universe,
with man the microcosm at the center. After
Hildegard of Bingen—12th century.

Much of what we have been saying with regard to St. George, the primordial creative act, initiation, the Grail legends and so on, is reiterated with a somewhat different emphasis in certain traditions which have grown up around the Archangel Michael. In the *Book of Revelation*, for instance, the defeat of the dragon is linked to events on a cosmic, apocalyptic plane resulting in the utter transformation of the created order. At the risk of sounding self-contradictory, we might say that at very high degrees of spiritual understanding and esoteric experience all intermediary degrees, planes and worlds are abolished and a direct link is achieved between human consciousness and Divine Being. To an extent, the seven-headed dragon correlates with the seven heavens and spheres of being as articulated in traditional cosmology and anthropology. Michael, the wielder of the axial lance or sword, who chases out the dragon from heaven, thus becomes the agent of a mystical transformation.

Furthermore, it is this function as enabler of the interchange of spiritual energies between the worlds that accounts for the patronage of St. Michael to so many sacred sites. Michael is particularly associated with those types of geographical features, such as certain hilltops, springs and caves, which in a symbolic landscape are perceived as nodes or centers where ingress and egress to other worlds and powers may be gained. We note finally the iconographical assimilation of the axial spear of the Archangel to the axial Cross of Christ so often seen in depictions of Michael fighting the dragon.

These few pages represent barely a fragment of the immense file dealing with the complex and important symbolism of the Cosmic Axis. We have, however, dug deep enough to at least begin to see the practical ramifications of the axial symbolism.

A very general overview of the Axis, then, reveals three primary characteristics of immediate importance:

1)The Axis is a vertical channel or pivotal line which joins, transfixes, and binds the Worlds. It is thus symbolically, the "spindle" of creation around which the whole cosmic order revolves.

2)The Axis, especially as it is expressed in certain images like the Tree, Ladder, Cross, or Body of Christ, functions as a *via sancta*, a holy way, often providing a very specific itinerary for the initiate's passage between the worlds and planes of being.

3)The Axis likewise functions as a conduit through which spiritual energies flow between the worlds and planes.

An exploration of the experiential significance of this triad of axial structures is undertaken in the practical work which follows.

Exercise:
THE LANCE OF LIGHT

Using *the Kenotic Opening*, enter the deep peace. Begin to recite the ritual phrase for *the Sphere of Creation* exercise and, as you do this, be aware of the sphere of light building around you. The sphere expands, its light separating until you are aware of innumerable stars flashing upon the great indigo globe of the heavens.

The landscape solidifies: You are standing upon the summit of a great mountain, and you are aware of the stream flowing nearby.

In the distance you see starlight glinting off the surface of a great sea. Looking toward the horizon, you become aware of a rising star. Following the movement of this star, you raise your vision until you gaze upon the pole star high above. And, as you meditate upon this pivotal point, you are suddenly aware of a ray of light shooting forth from it, descending with lightning speed to envelope you in a mighty pillar of light.

The pillar passes through the very center of the earth until it stretches from one pole of the cosmos to the other. You are aware of yourself within this luminous column and find your spiritual vision is heightened.

You become aware of the great cosmic dance, of subtle currents of spiritual force at play within the universe and of the hierarchy of spiritual beings. You are conscious of petals of rainbow light descending—like manna from heaven—within the column toward you. Some of the petals pass within you, providing nourishment for your soul. Others move by you and disappear into the depths below. You allow your gaze to follow them and perceive the crystals within the earth. As you gaze upon the shining gemstones beneath you, you are reminded of the lights of the stars above—to which you now return your attention.

The landscape fades from vision. The sphere contracts drawing the stars closer together into a bright orb of pure starlight. The axis grows thinner too, until it is as a narrow spear of infinite length running through the poles of the aura-sized orb surrounding you. You are in effect, "transfixed" by a lance of light passing through your spinal column. You meditate upon this, chanting to yourself the chosen ritual phrase (*suggestions*: "A piercing ray of deepest peace;" "Blessed are those transfixed by peace;" "Be hallowed by a piercing ray.").

III

the
holy fire

The great German Theosopher, Jacob Boehme, wrote that at the creation of the universe "the unchangeable God moved himself toward fire and light and stirred up the fire-property."[107] More than two thousand years earlier, Heraclitus of Ephesus had also spoken of fire as the primal element of the cosmos.[6] In Norse mythology, the fire giant, Surt, wields his flaming sword at the beginning and end of all creation.[101] Indeed, many divine beings are closely associated with fire. The Hindu god Agni, for example, has flaming hair and, being reborn every time a new fire is kindled, remains eternally young.[30] In the *Bhagavadgita*, Krishna is described as "flaming all around."[7] In Old Testament tradition, God appeared to Moses in the form of a burning bush *(Exodus 3:21)*. During the dedication of Solomon's Temple, "fire came down from heaven...and the glory of the Lord filled the temple" *(2 Chronicles 7:1)*. A BuddhistSutra relates how once when Gautama meditated in a cave the place was illumined by his fiery ecstasy.[37] And according to *The Gospel of Thomas* Jesus said, "Who is near me is near the fire."[95]

As this brief, but varied, glimpse into world traditions suggests, the symbolism of fire is complex and wide ranging. It is far beyond the scope of this chapter to deal with the many details that make up the enormous dossier on sacred fire. We shall, therefore, confine our comments to a few themes which are likely to be of immediate practical value.

The fiery Christ blessing the cosmos
at the creation. After Hildegard of
Bingen.

Our aims are:

 a) to outline, in general, the significance of the holy fire in Magical Christianity; and

 b) to highlight certain features of what might be called "Christian *kundalini*," as it involves the invocation or arousal of the divine fire within the initiate.

As always, whenever we seek the deeper issues of Esotericism, we find ourselves immersed in traditional lore. In a legend collected in Persia by Marco Polo,[93, 26] fire is connected with a magical stone given the Three Magi after they brought the myrrh, frankincense and gold to the Christ Child at Bethlehem. According to this story the Magi received, in exchange for their gifts, a small casket containing a stone. On their journey home they cast the stone into a well of immense depth and immediately fire descended from heaven into that well, then roared up in a blaze that lit the sky. The Magi were amazed. Aware that here was something great and holy, they took a spark of the fire and brought it back to their own country. There, inside a magnificent church, the fire was kept perpetually burning.

This simple legend is replete with several layers of esoteric significance. Note the presence of the Four Elements : *earth*, represented by the stone; *water* by the well; *air*, the medium through which the *fire* passes; and *fire* itself. The fire originates in the celestial world. Its path of descent traces along the line of the World Axis. In fact, one of the symbolic functions of the well is to complete the line of the Axis by being the channel through which the holy fire passes into the underworld thereby conjoining the lower with the celestial and middle realms. There is, then, a representation not only of the Four Elements, that is, the essential constituents and root qualities of creation, but also of the Three Worlds or regions that define the cosmos in a vertical plane. Furthermore, there is a precise relationship between the fire and the stone. In addition to being an image of the element of earth, the stone represents a cosmic center, or rather *the* Cosmic Center, the heart of the Mystical Body of Christ. The divine fire with its origins in the realm of the heavens and its destination as the Cosmic Center brings about the fusion of all beings, worlds, elements, powers and energies. All are united within the Center, all are infused with the living fire of the Holy Spirit.

In our next chapter we shall see how the Cosmic Center, the "Heart of God," and the human heart are linked through a series of symbolic resonances. For the moment, however, let us mark the close relationship between the holy fire and the heart— a relationship which depends in part upon the shared symbolism of spiritual love. The English hermit, Richard Rolle, writes of his experience of the inner fire in the *Incendium Amoris* :

> I cannot tell you how surprised I was the first time I felt my heart begin to warm. It was a real warmth too, not imaginary, and it felt as if it were actually on fire. ... I had to keep feeling my breast to make sure there was no physical reason for it! But once I realized it came entirely from within, that this fire of love had no cause, material or sinful but was the gift of my Maker, I was absolutely delighted, and wanted my love to be even greater....It set my soul aglow as if a real fire was burning there.[94.]

The Holy Spirit descends at Pentecost, resting as flames of fire upon the heads of Mary and the Apostles.

Meister Eckhart, in a powerful passage, also writes of fiery love, but as a force which suffused the cosmos at the Crucifixion: "On the Cross his Heart burnt like a fire and a furnace from which the flame burst forth on all sides. So was he inflamed on the Cross by his fire of love for the whole world."[103] The perspectives represented by these two authors—the personal and the universal—are quite complementary. For as we shall repeatedly see, the arousal of the holy fire within the Christian initiate amounts to nothing less than an *imitatio Christi*.

But the fire of divine love is also the fire of holy wisdom: "And he gave me a goblet filled with fire, and when I had drunk it wisdom grew in me ...." says an apocryphal book of Ezra.[28, 2] There is a legend in which St. Thomas touches the wound in the side of Christ (i.e. the Heart) and draws forth fire.† Thomas is, of course, the great "gnostic," the one who sought direct knowl-

†In a related legend, it is John standing nearby who catches the blood which runs after Thomas' touch, and soaks it into some bread kept over from the Last Supper. This was kept as a healing unction, and used to bless the Host.

edge of the divine wisdom, and the one who came to know it by touching the fiery heart of Christ.   Fire as a symbol of the direct transmission of holy wisdom is one of the initiatory keys of Magical Christianity. To the prepared soul the experience of the *hagia sophia* brings, amongst much else, a direct knowledge of the relatedness of all things. In the tradition of Pentecost, when the divine fire rests upon the Apostles, they are able to speak to any man in any tongue *(Acts 2:1-11)*. In other words, the spiritual barriers of separation are removed and they realize their relatedness to all beings. They are given a glimpse of the primordial wholeness. In specific mythological terms they are returned to the golden age before the Confusion of Tongues *(Genesis 11:1)*. To know a thing spiritually, then, is to realize one's profound relatedness to it and thereby, through the harmonic quality of consciousness, to realize one's relatedness to the totality of Cosmos and Creator. This experience places the Christian Mage in the role of mediator, capable, if willing, of acting as a channel for divine energies. For mediation is a direct outcome of attunement with spiritual reality.

Several of the methods used to tune consciousness in the Christian Mysteries today are, in fact, modifications of techniques well known in certain early Christian circles. The deliberate and conscious development, purification, and transformation of one's soul through the agency of divine fire is fairly well evidenced, for one, in the legends and visions of the Egyptian Desert Fathers:

Once, a monk went to see the hermit Abba Joseph and said, "Abba, according to my means I have accomplished my humble service, my humble fasting, my prayer, my meditation and my seclusion, according to my means I try to be pure in my thought. What more can I do?" Then Joseph stood up and spread his hands toward Heaven. His fingers became like ten flames of fire. And he said: "If you want to, you can become wholly like fire."[112]

On another occasion, a brother traveled to the cell of Abba Arsenius in the desert. When he arrived outside the door, he looked in the window and saw the old man as a great flame of fire.[112]

One day Mark the Egyptian was offering up a prayer at mass when he had a vision. An angel of the Lord descended from

The divine power breaks through the celestial plane, descending
in a fiery torrent to conceive the Divine Child within the Virgin.
Detail from a Russian Icon—*14th century.*

heaven and placed his hand upon the head of the presiding priest who became as a burning column of fire.[108]

Another desert monk, Constantine of Bethany, was reciting a psalm at Matins when his appearance was transformed into a great pillar of fire.[29]

The experience of the divine fire was not limited to individuals alone. According to *The Paradise of the Fathers*, when monks gathered to pray, they generated a column of fire that reached to heaven.[53]

As these accounts suggest, the holy fire represents not only the descent of spiritual power, but the means of ascent or attunement to the divine presence. "Not only is the Godhead brought down to man, but man is raised up to the Godhead." It will be observed that several of our examples focus on the image of a column or pillar of fire. In these instances the image of divine fire also functions as a symbol of the Universal Axis which, as we have said, is the channel through which spiritual energy moves between the worlds. Thus it is that columns and pillars have a particular significance in the founding and integral structure of many ancient churches.

An Armenian legend of St. Nino, tells how, after the king's builders failed numerous times to erect the pillar for a new church....

> St. Nino accompanied by twelve women from among her disciples remained by the column and wept. Then Nino arose and stretched out her arms in prayer to God, and said, "May this project on which the king is engaged not be brought to nothing." When dawn approached, the women fell asleep, but Nino stood with upraised hands. Suddenly there appeared by her a young man adorned with brilliant light and shrouded in fire. He spoke three words to her, at which she fell down upon her face. Then the youth touched the pillar with his hand and raised it, and it stood up. And the pillar blazed like a column of fire, and moved by itself to approach its base. There it stood twelve cubits above its pedestal, which had been carved for it out of the stump of that same cedar tree from which this Living Pillar was hewn out.
>
> At dawn the king got up in a mood of depression, and went to look at the garden and at the church which he had started to build with so much enthusiasm. Shooting up towards heaven from his garden he saw a light like a flash of lightning. He came running to the spot with all his followers and the townspeople who had also observed the marvel. Then the column, resplendent with light, descended on to its place as if from heaven, and stood firmly on its base without being touched by human hands.[62]

The legend refers to a fiery "Living Pillar" as the core and support of the holy edifice. In accordance with the esoteric doctrine of correspondences, ancient churches often replicate symbolically both the cosmic structure and the human constitution : body, soul and spirit. There is, then, an esoteric formula underpinning the legend of St. Nino which might be summarized as follows: World Axis = Tree of Life (Sacred Tree) = Fiery Pillar of Church = Spinal Column. The living pillar of fire, consecrated by the touch of the flame-being—here an angel or even possibly Christ—enables the building, and by extension the human being, to exist as a sacred site, a place where holy presence is manifest.

Let us also recall that angels are typically described as fiery beings. The foundational pillar or column of fire may thus also represent an angelic presence overseeing the sacred site. Here we have a glimpse into the reality behind the popular traditions of guardian or guiding angels. For these holy beings were probably originally associated with sacred places rather than with particular individual souls. This allows, of course, that an individual would have come under the protection and direction of the angelic presence associated with his or her place of worship.

The pillar of fire is an image which occurs in Christian mystical and magical tradition with some frequency. In Christian Mythology it finds its prototype in the Old Testament story of *Exodus*. The Israelites are guided into the promised land by a pillar of cloud during the day and a pillar of fire at night. Both these images came fairly early on to denote, interchangeably, the mystical ascent of the soul to God and the descent of divine energy into the soul. Over time the images came to signify two distinct, even opposing, approaches to mystical experience. The pillar of cloud became a root image—and this is somewhat paradoxical—for the *via negativa,* the way of negation, in which the soul rejects all images and attributes in its quest for God (The method is aptly described in an anonymous medieval manual titled *The Cloud of Unknowing.).* The pillar of fire, on the other hand, became a key symbol for the *via affirmativa,* that is, the way of affirmation, in which the soul seeks God through images and attributes.

Our concern at present, however, is less with mysticism (i.e. the quest for personal union with God), than it is with becoming a channel for the work of God; with becoming a mediator of spiritual energy to the world at large; with what Dionysios the Areopagate and others term "Theurgy."

Dionysios' writings date from the sixth century, but the tradition he represents dates from the time of Paul.† Dionysios is considered the great spokesman for the *via negativa.* To be sure, he was the first Christian Adept to write extensively of the divine darkness and the unknowability of God, but he also ably articulated a "metaphysics of light,"[97] and his works are filled with profound exegeses of symbols. Dionysios was well aware

---

†cf. *Acts 17:32* after Paul's talk on the Unknown God.

that the "promised land" was reached by following *both* the pillar of cloud *and* the pillar of fire. Dionysios says of fire:

> The Word of God seems to honor the depiction of fire above all others. You will find that it depicts not only flaming wheels, but also burning animals and even men who are somehow aglow. [25]

In writing of "men who are somehow aglow," Dionysios is drawing attention to long-standing traditions of the awakening of the holy fire within the Christian initiate. Elsewhere, he writes that "the power of fire causes a lifting up to the godlike."[25]

We have seen that the desert monks sought to attain the fiery state of illumination through ascetic practice. Yet the possibility of illumination, as an experience here and now, is itself fully present in the initiation rites—particularly before the church suppressed its own arcane disciplines. The rituals of illumination are mentioned in ancient texts in connection with several symbolic terms and images which are of interest to us here.

At least as early as the fourth century, inner visions relating to the descent and ascent of spiritual luminescence were deliberately induced during the initiation rites. A baptismal hymn written by Ephram the Syrian contains the following lines:

> O brothers, open your senses and contemplate
> the hidden column,
> whose base rests upon the waters
> and which rises to the celestial gate,
> like the ladder that Jacob saw.
> On it the light descends to the baptism,
> and the soul rises to heaven,
> so that all may be united in love.[29]

More detailed descriptions of the symbolism involved in the ancient initiatory visions are to be found embedded in the lives of certain saints. *The Acts of St. Marina*, for instance, also dat-

This 9th century cross contains several elements of initiatic significance. The hand of God appears bearing a crown from the fiery realm of the Spirit. At the right and left hand of Christ are the powers of sun and moon, while at the foot of the cross is a coiled dragon.

ing from the fourth century, contains some interesting elements.

One episode in particular, tells how St. Marina, having been condemned to die by drowning, prayed that her chains be broken and that the water serve as her sanctification and initiation into the baptismal mystery. Then she addressed the Risen Christ, saying, "O eternal one, may you envelop me with your spirit, with your holy garment." And straight away there descended from heaven a dove bearing a crown in its beak. Then the chains of the saint fell away as she stood up in the water, praising and glorifying God. The dove darted quickly to Marina and touched her lightly and said to her. "Peace be with you, servant of Jesus. Take heart, for in this moment you are to be crowned." The dove extended its wings and flew out of the water. And a column of fire appeared from heaven, and above it was a cross. Marina gave thanks and exclaimed, "The Lord is become my king, he is shrouded in beautiful garments. You are my illumination, Jesus Christ, O Rabbi, Adonai, I have been freed by the light of the Lord. You have glorified me, Lord Jesus, you have justified me,

Christ, and you have clothed me with your holy vestment."[29]

The story of Marina's experience accords with what we know of the ancient rites. Not only is the central theme one of liberation or salvation, but in terms of the actual rubrics of baptism, we know that candidates were crowned and received new vestments in the form of white robes (white symbolizing light, purity, illumination, and other qualities characterized by sacred fire).†

Let us also recall that the baptized were often known as *illuminati*, and that their experience of illumination was undoubtedly bound up with the consonant symbolism of water and fire.‡ John Climacus reveals an awareness of the occult connection between these two elements when he remarks how those who have attained to the "angelic state" become "incorruptible"—they no longer desire food and cannot become sick—because they are "sustained by a celestial fire" which is just like "an underground stream that nourishes the root of a plant."[13]

According to Persian tradition, *kavarenah,* the vital fire or radiance that pervades and enables all life, rises through the medium of water into all animals, plants, and humans. In the latter it is said to concentrate in the head whence it radiates a glowing light. This is the origin of the nimbus, or halo, that shines about the heads of the saints.[28]

The correlation between the holy fire and the "angelic state" of illumination also figures strongly in the legend of the *Martyrdom of Theodorus*. According to this tradition the saint had a vision of a ladder that rose from the depths of the earth to the heights of heaven. An enormous dragon lived at the foot of the ladder. At the top was a mighty figure sitting on a magnificent throne, around which were a myriad of flaming beings. The one

---

†The use of white robes specifically reflects the initiate's spiritual participation in the Mystery of the Transfiguration: "And His face shone like the sun, and His garments became as white as light" (Matthew 17:2). In the realm of symbolic structures light and fire are often synonymous images.

‡Liturgically, the relationship between the two elements is epitomized in the ritual mixing of the water and wine (liquid fire) which is itself linked both to the flow of water and blood from Christ's side at the Crucifixion, and to Christ's changing of water into wine at Cana. The latter episode, significantly, is celebrated at the Feast of the Epiphany—along with Easter and Pentecost, one of the three days traditionally set aside for the initiation rites.

The fiery serpent of *Numbers 21:4-9* with which
Christ identified himself. From a 16th century
amulet for protection against the plague.

who was seated on the throne said to Theodorus, "Do you want
to be my child?" Theodorus said, "Who are you, Lord?" "I am
Jesus the Logos of God; your blood will be soon spilt in my name."
Then Theodorus was lifted up and baptized with the baptism of
fire. He was taken to the Lake of Fire and plunged in three
times; and he became wholly of fire like those who are gathered
about the throne.[29]

This vision, occurring just before his martyrdom, was given
in preparation for Theodorus' entry to the celestial realms. It
contains three key symbols or motifs: the ladder, the dragon,
and the baptism by fire. The ladder as it relates to the Cosmic
Axis, the Cross, and the Mystical Body of Christ has been treated
in our previous chapter. The symbol of the dragon and its corollary the serpent we have also looked at from the perspective of
pre-cosmic force. There is however another less well known, and
certainly esoteric, aspect to the figure of the serpent or dragon—

During the Middle Ages crosiers like the one at left were commonly wrought in the shape of serpents or dragons. On one level, based on the words of Jesus in Matthew. 10:16, "Be ye therefore wise as serpents.," they are symbols of saintly wisdom. On another and obviously related level, the crosier signifies the spiritual authority of one who has been granted mastery over the personal and cosmic energies of the serpent power or holy fire.

its role as a symbol of the Axis itself. There is a Jewish midrash *(Berashith Rabba 68)*, for instance, which identifies the dragon with Jacob's ladder by way of which the angels ascend and descend to rescue the souls of the dead. The New Testament assigns the symbol of the fiery serpent to Christ himself: "And as Moses lifted up the serpent in the wilderness, so must the Son of man be lifted up"*(John 3:14)*. The serpent which Moses lifted up refers to an Old Testament story which relates how the Israelites were attacked by fiery serpents. "So Moses prayed for the people. And the lord said to Moses, 'Make a fiery serpent, and set it on a pole; and every one who is bitten, when he sees it, shall live'" *(Numbers 21:4-9)*.

In practical esoteric terms the fiery serpent/dragon force must be "crucified," raised up, that it may open the higher modes of awareness, enabling the initiate to perceive directly the nature of spiritual reality.

An alternative model for this process is the baptism of fire.

After Theodorus is immersed thrice in the Lake of Fire, he becomes "wholly of fire" like the angels about the throne. Esoterically speaking, the threefold immersion represents, *inter alia*, the candidate's initiation into the mysteries of the three worlds; his passage through the three "ages of man"—a symbolic completion of the rounds of birth and death; and his ritual enactment of the three days of Christ in the tomb preceding the Resurrection.

According to *The Celestial Hierarchy,* the angels nearest the divine throne or Center are the *Seraphim.* This is the word translated as "fiery serpents" in the passage from *Numbers* quoted above. Dionysios translates the word as both "those who are on fire," and "makers of fire." In the Dionysian tradition the term *Seraphim* designates on one hand, the fiery nature of the angelic beings themselves and on the other, their power to illuminate others.[25] The purpose of the baptism of fire, then, is to transmute the soul by raising it to an angelic vibration. It signifies both a mystical and personally transformative vision, and also the awakening and arousal within the initiate of the capacity to mediate the holy power of illumination.

The baptism of fire is a motif found frequently in the ancient visions, and invariably takes place in either a lake or river of fire. Occasionally, as in *The Apocalypse of Bartholomew,* the two images of fiery lake and flaming river occur together.

According to this legend, the Apostle Thomas revived his son Siophanes who had lain dead for seven days. Siophanes, then related how his soul had journeyed through the heavens under

Ancient tradition associates the Christ with the phoenix, that mythical bird which resurrects periodically through the agency of fire.

The Baptism of Christ in the Jordan. A column of light descends from the celestial world, drawing the waters up around the body of Jesus. Note the flames in the water. From an illustrated manuscript of Gregory Nazianzen's *On the Holy Light*.

the conduct of the Archangel Michael. He was led through the celestial regions with the angels singing before him. They came to a river of fire, Michael took him by the hand, and led him into the river, whereupon Siophanes became like a flaming fire. Afterwards the Archangel brought him to a lake of fire and immersed him three times in its waters. Then a voice sounded out of the heights bidding the angels to conduct him to the celestial paradise.[29, 2]

From the point of view of esoteric function, the lake of fire and the river of fire are synonymous images—as are their biblical prototypes, the Red Sea and the Jordan River. In *The Old Jordan* both constitute liberation from an oppressive or unfulfilled mode of existence. It is partly for this reason that these myths were invoked during the Christian rituals as paradigms of initiation. More importantly, the crossing of the Red Sea and the crossing of the Jordan were invoked during the rites because they were also symbolically resonant with Jesus' own baptism in the Jordan.

We need hardly reiterate here the importance of the Baptism of Christ as a *leitmotif* in the early initiation ceremonies. What *is* worth noting, however, is the existence of several ancient references clearly linking the Baptism in the Jordan with holy fire. In the second century, for example, Justin wrote: "When Jesus had descended into the water, the Jordan was set on fire."[29]† When touched by the Divine Being elemental water is transformed into spiritual fire. The fiery river and lake might thus be termed the spiritual octaves of the Jordan and the Red Sea. They sound the same notes on a higher level. As the tales of Theodorus and Siophanes show, the baptism of fire is an experience of profound purification and transformation that prepares one for the knowledge of the upper worlds, the celes

Training in a Christian Mystery School aims at bringing out latent talents and abilities to be used in service to the inner orders of Saints and Adepts under the Christ. Since the occult energies which are embodied in the image of fire are by nature creative, magical forces emanating from Divine Being and catcion

†The tradition is given from a slightly different angle in *The Chronicon Pascal* which remarks how, when Jesus came out of the water at the Baptism, "The heavens were straight-away opened and the Holy Ghost came in the shape of a dove resembling fire...."

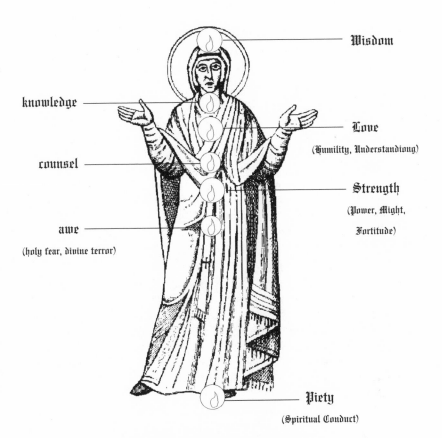

Wisdom

knowledge

Love

(Humility, Understandiong)

counsel

Strength

(Power, Might,

Fortitude)

awe

(holy fear, divine terror)

Piety

(Spiritual Conduct)

The "Gifts of the Spirit" are usually numbered seven. These may be subdivided into two groups of three with the gift of Piety (spiritual conduct) as the working out of the other gifts on the physical plane. Love , Wisdom, and Power thus constitute the Greater Triad; counsel, knowledge, and awe comprise the Lesser Triad. In the Illustration above, the Seven Gifts are shown in the context of the seven centers of occult and mystical physiology. These spiritual centers have (somewhat fluid) connections to certain organs and regions of the physical body. In this case: crown, throat, heart, solar plexus, navel, genitals, and feet.

tial hierarchy, and the stages of being leading to the Godhead. It is, in short, the higher octave of the baptism of water and constitutes an initiation within the initiation, reserved for those able and willing to receive it.

Furthermore, the arousal within the initiate of the holy fire, the purpose of which is the attainment or awakening of the "Resurrection Body" is firmly based upon an exemplary pattern laid down by Christ's Baptism in the Jordan. Origen puts it succinctly thus "In the baptism of water, we are entombed with Christ; in the baptism of fire, we are configured to his glorious body."[21, 72] Here we are reminded of the legend of St. Marina and how the Christ appeared to her vested in fire. But other traditions are even more explicit.

In his chapter on *The Mystery of Illumination*, Dionysios remarks how Christ descended "like a fire," making "one with himself all those capable of being divinized."[25] James of Sarug(500) says "How marvelous and astonishing it is to relate how the fire, enveloped in a body, was baptized in the water and how the high flame-being... descended into the Jordan to be laved."[87] Finally, a Syrian text describes the moment of Jesus' Baptism as follows, "There is a spark in the water, a flame glideth up and down in the wave. God is being laved in the Jordan."[87] It is precisely because the Christ takes the form of fire that the Christian initiate seeks to arouse the holy fire within himself. By becoming attuned to the spiritual symbolism of fire, one becomes attuned to Universal Being, and to the flow of Divine Love, Wisdom, and Power between the worlds. One thus becomes capable—especially if skilled in the use of intercessory ritual, prayer, and meditation— of acting as a channel for archetypal energies.†

Training in a Christian Mystery School aims at bringing our latent talents and abilities to be used in service to the inner orders of Saints and Adepts under the Christ. Since the occult energies which are embodied in the image of fire are by nature creative, magical forces emanating from the Divine Being and residing in the cosmos and the soul, their arousal can result in

†This is, however, rarely the glamorous work it is sometimes thought to be. Archetypal patterns are usually worked out in the apparently quite unexciting daily life of the initiate. Mediation often takes place unseen, without fanfare, praise, acknowledgment, or understanding from those around one.

the manifestation of certain psychic phenomena, or in the awakening in the individual of gifts, virtues, and powers. As attested in all the Esoteric Traditions, such an awakening may also entail some temporary emotional turbulence as the newly released inner energies find their level—though this is minimized by dedication to a higher cause. The exercise which follows is quite safe, therefore, if undertaken with the intention of arousing one's potential for use in service to Divine Being, and if kept within the context of the entire series of exercises given in this book.

Exercise:
THE LIVING FLAME

Having performed *the Kenotic Opening*, begin to recite the ceremonial phrase for *the Sphere of Creation*. As you do this, be aware of a luminous sphere building around you.

Feel the sphere expanding. And as the sphere grows, its light separates into innumerable points that flash as stars upon the indigo darkness of the celestial orb.

The landscape forms about you. You stand upon the plateau at the summit of the mountain. Near you runs the stream and in the distance you catch the glint of starlight on the surface of a great sea.

Next, recite the phrase for *the Lance of Light* and become aware of the axis of light running through the poles of the sphere and through the line of your spinal column.

Be aware of the crystals within the earth, and of their celestial counterparts, the stars above.

Now reach your consciousness upwards, beyond the pole of the cosmic sphere, up towards the source of absolute illumination.

Become aware, out of this infinite light, of the figure of a dove descending towards you along the line of the axis of light. The dove gradually assumes the form of a river of golden fire. And the fire shoots down passing through your spinal column like a rushing wind or waterfall.

Having descended deep into the heart of the earth, it kindles there a secret spiritual flame. The stream of fire then turns back and slowly begins to rise up the shaft of the axis towards you. It enters the base of your spinal column and rushes up to your head, flowing into your cranium, filling your mind with bright, golden fire.

You feel your head transformed into a blazing disk of light with tongues of flame shooting upward from it like the peaks of a crown.

A shower of golden sparks now begins to fall from your head, forming a pool of golden light at your feet. This rises about you in a great tide. You are immersed in a wondrous sea of golden fire.

This sea of light gradually fades. And you become aware that your entire body has become transfigured into a golden flame of divine spirit....

The fire recedes, slowly emptying through your feet, then moves back down the axis. The fire briefly merges with the flame at the center of the earth, whereupon the crystals within the land flash momentarily like a blanket of stars.

The stream of living fire passes through the earth. As it nears the opposite pole of the cosmos, it resumes the form of a white dove and is once again received into the light of the Absolute.

The sphere contracts, drawing the stars together until they merge again into one sphere of pure star light. And you are aware also of the lance of infinite length running through your spinal column and through the poles of the aura-sized sphere by which you are encompassed.

And still glowing, deep within the cave of your heart is a bright spark of the golden fire brought by the dove of spirit. You meditate upon the significance of this living flame. And as you do so, you repeat over to yourself, the relevant ceremonial phrase (*suggestions*: "A holy fount of living fire;" "Blessed are those who raise up the Fire;" "Be hallowed by a living fire.").

ÍO

the
CENTER

Most traditional cultures claim one or more sacred sites as marking a central "heart" or "navel" of the world. For the Kogi of northwestern Colombia, for instance, the entire range of the Sierra Nevada is located at the heart of the cosmos. Not only collectively, but also individually, the mountains are seen to give access to the Center. Man was born on the summit of a mountain and to this place of origin his soul returns at death. Moreover, the mountains are perceived as reflecting the very structure of the universe, and this structure is in turn mirrored in the architecture of the ceremonial lodge. Each lodge is marked by openings to the four directions and from the midpoint of the conical roof hangs a thread which connects the peak to the navel of the Earth Mother. The Kogi also encounter the Mother in caves representing the Cosmic Womb.[92]

We have mentioned already (Chapter i) the connection between the ceremonial *kivas* of the Pueblo Indians of New Mexico and the Cosmic Womb. In the Tewa Pueblo of San Juan, there exists a circle of stones known as the "earth mother earth navel middle place." Though now located in the south plaza, the Earth Mother Navel was at one time located inside a circular *kiva*. This central navel is both the place of origins and the source for continued life. It is from here the people first emerged into this world. Here too is the source of "blessings" which radiate outward across the land. The blessings are gathered in by a set of

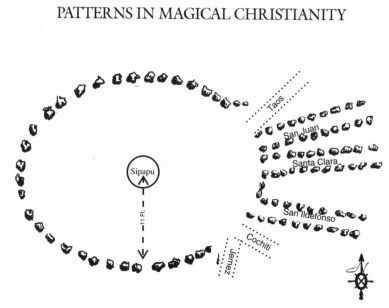

One of the earth navels of the Tewa Cosmos. At the peak of Mt. Chicoma, sacred mountain of the West, is a circle of stones with channels opening toward the Tewa Pueblos. At the center is a *sipapu*, a shallow depression signifying a place of access to the otherworlds.

secondary earth navels (also composed of stones, but shaped like keyholes or open wombs) on the four sacred mountains and redirected towards the various Tewa villages. Furthermore, all the earth navels in the Tewa cosmos are points of intersection between the three cosmic regions (over, under, and middle).[88]

What is useful about our knowledge of the Kogi and Tewa worlds is that they demonstrate the function and structure of the Center within the context of a complete symbolic cosmos. Human and divine beings, architecture and the sacred landscape all have intense correlations, all are entwined in a set of meaningful relations through their connection to the Center. It is obvious we are dealing with notions that are extremely ancient and widespread and which have their basis in a perception of the cosmos as the "garment" of the Sacred. Certain features in the landscape are capable of revealing or giving access to the deeper or higher mysteries of being and creation. In almost every tradition, the Center is associated with a sacred mountain, tree, stone, spring, or cave.

Christ at the navel of the world. He stands atop the
sacred stone/mountain from which flow the four world
rivers. Next to him is the "Lamb of God." Two palm trees
are behind him. The one to his right, in which can be
seen a phoenix, probably represents the Tree of Life.

According to Taoist tradition, the world mountain, *k'un-lun,*
is some three thousand miles high. There may be found the fountain of immortality and thence flow the four great world rivers.
Its slopes are of gold and silver and precious stones, and on it, at
the Center of the Universe, reside the Four Kings of Heaven.[64]

In Christian tradition Paradise, "the place where the earth
joins the sky,"[111] is an inaccessible garden surrounded by a fiery
wall that reaches to the heavens. "Here is the tree of life which
gives immortality, here is the fountain which divides into four
streams that go forth to water the world."[111] Christian tradition
also often places Paradise on a mountain. For Godfrey of Viterbo
(1186), for example, Paradise is "a golden mountain redolent
with wonderful odors and adorned with an image of Virgin and
Child."[111] In Dante's *Divine Comedy,* the earthly paradise is located upon the peak of Mount Purgatory. This peak is formed of
earth that, before being displaced as a result of the Fall, was
originally at the exact center of the terrestrial orb.[23]

Two renditions of the Delphic *omphalos.*

For the Samaritans, Gerizim is known as *eres tabbur*, "the navel of the earth." It is the holy mountain where God created Adam, where Noah landed in his ark, where Isaac was bound by Abraham, where Jacob dreamed of his ladder and set up a sacred stone, where patriarchs are buried and where Moses looked as he lay dying nearby.[15]

In *The Book of Jubilees* (8:19) we are told that "the Garden of Eden is the holy of holies, and the dwelling of the Lord, and Mount Sinai the center of the desert and Mount Zion the center of the navel of the earth...." The two mountains, Sinai and Zion (Mount Moriah), represented for the ancient Israelites places where the Center of the universe could be found. In pre-Davidic times, Sinai was the pre-eminent node, for it was here Yahweh gave the Law to Moses. After the establishment of Jerusalem as the capital of the Kingdom the divine presence at Mt. Sinai became accessible at Mt. Zion, and Zion assumed many of the attributes of Sinai.[15]

In ancient Greece, the Center manifested in the form of a sacred stone known as the *omphalos* (literally "navel"). Most important was the *omphalos* at the temple of Apollo at Delphi.†
The site was determined when two eagles, sent out by Zeus, one from the east, the other from the west, met at this spot. Alternatively, according to Peloponesian myth, when the goddess Harmonia wove the fabric of the universe, "she first represented the earth with its omphalos in the center."[64]

†According to Plato, Apollo is the god who "sits upon the stone at the center of the earth" *(Republic 427b).*

The development of the traditions of the Foundation Stone at Jerusalem was influenced both by the Hellenistic conceptions of the omphalos and by the indigenous traditions of Palestine and Syria where sacred stones were also numerous. Known as *baetyls* or *bethels*, there were famous examples at the Temple of El Gabel in Emesa and in a mountain top shrine near Antioch, to name but two.[98] In the Old Testament the place where Jacob laid his head upon a stone and dreamt of a ladder reaching to Heaven became known as *Bethel* (*Genesis 28:11-19*). The Foundation Stone itself was located at the site of the Holy of Holies in Solomon's Temple. Now housed by the Dome of the Rock, it consists of a roughly rectangular slab with a cave inside.

Thrones, being developments of *omphaloi* or sacred stones, are closely linked to the symbolism of the Center.
The Throne of St. Mark, Venice, shown at right, is carved with several nodal images including the Tree of Life, the Four World Rivers, and the Cross.

There is a whole assemblage of important symbols connected to the Foundation Stone: In Islamic tradition, at the end of time the *Kaaba* will fuse with the Foundation Stone.[106] Moreover, the cave within the stone, known as the "well of souls" is the place from where Mohammed ascended to Paradise.[9]

According to Rabinnic tradition:

> Just as the navel is found at the center of a human being, so the land of Israel is found at the center of the world

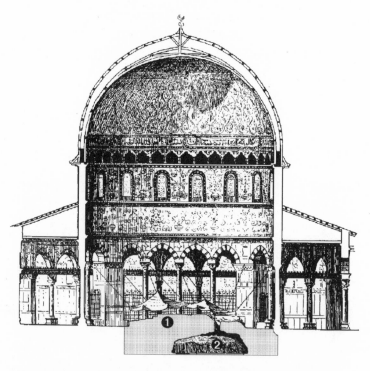

The Dome of the Rock, built upon the site of Solomon's Temple. The key feature of the site is the Foundation Stone ❶ with its sacred cave ❷. The site is closely allied to the origins of the Order of the Knights of the Temple whose esoteric rites were undoubtedly concerned with invoking the spiritual power of the Center.

... and it is the foundation of the world. Jerusalem is at the
center of the land of Israel, the Temple is at the center of
Jerusalem, the Holy of Holies is at the center of the Temple,
the Ark is at the center of the Holy of Holies and the Foundation Stone is in front of the Ark, which spot is the foundation
of the world.[99]

Moreover, for the Israelites, the Foundation Stone is where
Yahweh stood at the beginning of time; where Adam was created and buried; where Abraham shared in the mystic bread
and wine with Melchizedek; where Jacob had his dream-vision.
It is also the lid to the entrance to the underworld and from it
the primal light flowed at the creation.[99] In the New Testament, Christ is connected to the traditions of the Foundation
Stone when he is called the "Chief corner-stone," the "living
stone, ... chosen and precious." And it is the loss of the Center
that is being alluded to when Christ is referred to as the stone
which the builders rejected *(1Peter 2:1-7, Ephesians 3:21-22, Acts
4:11)*.

Images of the Center abound in Christianity. It is well known
to biblical scholars that Jerusalem plays a central role in parts
of the New Testament, especially the Lukan and Johannine
writings. In *Luke* and *Acts*, Jerusalem is the central reference
point. All the important events are placed in relation to Jerusalem.[55] In *Luke*, the movement is generally towards Jerusalem,
that is, towards the place where the central sacred events will
occur. In *Acts*, the movement is generally away from Jerusalem,
the Apostles go forth into the world bearing with them the teaching and power originally bestowed upon them and periodically
renewed for them at the heart of the world. In the Johannine
writings, the emphasis is on the New Jerusalem—an imaginal
symbol of the Center.

The relationship between the spiritual Center and its physical and imaginal symbols is of great import for Esoteric Christian practice and requires at least a brief elaboration. It would
be useful at this point, therefore, to underscore the distinction
between the *Center* and the *nodes*. The Center is a spiritual reality. It is what Plato calls a divine idea or form, and what Au-
gustine refers to as an archetype. There is no one sacred site,

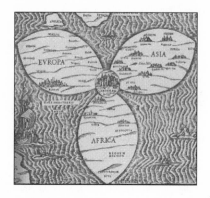

Medieval maps showing Jerusalem at the center of the world.

This early Christian mosaic floor depicts the celestial archetype of the earthly paradise. The night sky teeming with constellations resonates with the Garden of Eden teeming with fauna and flora. Four celestial rivers flow forth from the center of the starry heavens just as four world rivers flow forth from the center of the paradisal realm. The star at the center of the cosmic dome is mirrored in the stone, Tree of Life, or spring at the center of the earthly paradise.

symbol, or image which can contain or reveal the total power and significance of the Center. This is why there can be more than one place or image designated as the center of the world, even within the same tradition. The sites and symbols of the Center —whether they be physical places like Mt. Gerizim, Jerusalem, and Golgotha or imaginal constructs like *k'un-lun*, the New Jerusalem, and the Sacred Heart of Jesus—are merely nodes, gateways giving access to something which is otherwise inaccessible.

Let us reiterate. The Center is neither primarily a geographic site nor a geometric point, but a spiritual principle. Though it may be accessed through specialized nodes in sacred landscapes (whether physical or imaginal), and though we may gain a circumstantial understanding of its significance through geometric symbolism, the Center must not be confused with these expressions.

The spiritual significance of the Center transcends its physical and imaginal manifestations. This is why early maps have a tendency to be diagrammatic and symbolic rather than literal and physically accurate. The physical imprecision is not due merely to a lack of geographic knowledge, but to participation in a symbolic cosmos, a world in which reality is gauged more by fullness of meaning and spiritual power, than by quantitative measurement. Thus in many ancient European maps, Jerusalem is positioned at the center, not so much because it was considered the central point in the circle of a flat world, but because it was the most sacred place on earth.

A similar perspective might be assumed when we read the accounts of pilgrims to sacred sites. An Icelandic traveler, Nicholas of Thverva, made a pilgrimage to the Holy Land in the twelfth century. Of the Holy Sepulcher he wrote: "the center of the World is there; there, on the day of the summer solstice, the light of the sun falls perpendicularly from heaven."[35] But the sun doesn't actually fall straight down over the Sepulcher, for Jerusalem is about nine degrees north of the Tropic of Cancer. Another pilgrim to Jerusalem, Melito of Sardis (ca. 160 AD.), insists that the site of Christ's crucifixion lay at the "center of the city."[51] Golgotha was in fact located just outside the walls of Jerusalem during the time of Christ, and it is in this location also that Melito would have viewed it in the second century. There is probably neither ignorance, duplicity, nor delusion involved in these accounts. When powerful spiritual forces touch the soul, the physical world can be, and sometimes is, transfigured. The cosmos assumes a perfect form, one wholly in accord with the structure of spiritual reality. Far from being an hallucination or wishful daydream this is a kind of deep spiritual vision. One sees things not only as they should be, but as they really are *in potentia*. Nicholas of Thverva may have really seen the sun shining perpendicularly at the solstice and Melito of Sardis may have actually perceived Golgotha to be at the center of Jerusalem.†

Whatever one's opinion of the experiences of Nicholas and Melito, however, the sites which they visited, the Mount of the Crucifixion, and the Tomb of Christ, are both powerful nodes with highly developed traditions relating to the Center. There are certain Christian legends that place the tomb of Adam beneath the Mount of Golgotha. Origen was aware of these, as was Basil of Caesurea *(d. 349)*. The latter remarks that the skull of Adam was hidden beneath the hill upon which Christ was crucified.[17] In the Syrian *Book of the Cave of Treasures,* we read that Adam was created and buried at the center of the earth, on the same site where the Cross of Christ was later erected. As a result, Christ's blood fell upon the skull of the First Man, redeeming him, and thus making redemption possible for all humanity.[38] There is a kinship here with Paul's doctrine of Christ as the New Adam, the primal ancestor and exemplar who comes at the beginning of the New Creation.

As remarked, Golgotha was not the only site to be seen as a world center by the Christians. Near it lay the Holy Sepulcher, the place where Christ was buried, where he descended to the underworld and whence he emerged resurrected. When Christianity was allowed public reclamation of its holy sites in Jerusalem in the fourth century, tradition dictated that the Lord was buried in a cave beneath what had long been a temple of the goddess Venus. It was this that became the site for the church of the Holy Sepulcher—a fact which serves to emphasize the concordance between the Divine Feminine and the Cosmic Center.

The sacred cave is, in and of itself, a symbol of the Center. As we have already noted the cave is symbolic of the place of cosmic origins, the womb of creation. But it is also a place where

†Such experiences always involve a certain merging of planes and by nature present peculiar difficulties for expression and understanding. It is an all too common occurrence, even among trained esotericists for an experience of a fusion of the planes to lead to one's permanently confusing the planes. Thus the ability to discriminate among things is traditionally ranked one of the more important qualities an initiate should cultivate. Whether Nicholas and Melito both erred in taking a spiritual vision for a physical one, however, is unclear for several reasons—not the least of which is the simple fact that they lived in a *milieu* where the planes were closer together than is the case in our modern era.

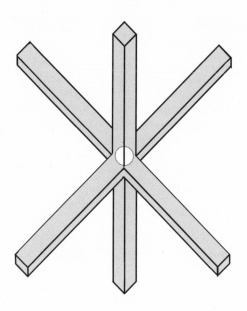

The ancient symbols of six-pointed cross and Monogram of Christ both incorporate the pattern of a three-dimensional cross of creation streaming forth from the primordial Center.

access is gained to the Axis, and thus to all the worlds and planes of being. The Sepulcher was one of three sacred caves held most reverent by the early Christians. The others were the Cave of the Nativity, and the rarely mentioned Cave of the Ascension. It was, according to early traditions, from a cave near the summit of the Mount of Olives that Christ ascended.[51]

This same cave appears in a somewhat different context in an apocryphal gospel of John. The text relates how during the time of the Crucifixion, John goes to the Mount of Olives and enters a cave. There he sees the figure of Christ standing before him, his very presence illuminating the darkness of the cave. The Lord gives John a vision of a cross of light and speaks to him of its esoteric significance "This cross ... is that which joined all things unto itself by the word, ... and then also, being one, made all things flow forth."[2] Here we have the images of the mountain, the Cross, and the cave occurring together. More importantly, note that the Cross is that which both unites and enables creation.

There are a number of other important documents which mention this cosmic doctrine of the Cross. *The Clemetine Homilies*, for example, speak of the creation as follows:

> There proceeds from God, the heart of the world, indefinite extension—upwards and downwards, to the right and left, backward and forward. Looking in these six directions, as at a constant number, he completes the creation of the world, of which he is the beginning and the end. In him the six phases of time have their end, and it is from him that they receive their indefinite extension. And that is the secret of the number seven *(Homily xvii).* [108, 1]

In simple geometric terms, this passage demonstrates a set of cosmic relationships which are appropriately expressed in the symbol of the six-pointed cross so well known from early Christian inscriptions. This type of cross is also the underlying pattern for the *chi rho* or Monogram of Christ. It is a symbol that expresses creation as the development of a three dimensional cosmic cross out of the Divine Center, "the heart of the world," as Clement calls it.

The symbolism of the Cross as or at the Center is taken up from a different perspective in *The Acts of Peter*. Peter is crucified upside down in order to reverse the pattern of creation warped by the fall of Adam:

> Concerning which the Lord saith in a mystery: 'Unless ye make the things of the right hand as those of the left, and those of the left as those of the right, and those that are above as those below, and those that are behind as those that are before, ye shall not have knowledge of the kingdom.' [2]

Peter then remarks that the nail or pivot at the center of the cross represents "conversion," that is, it signifies a true change of heart. Naturally, we are not speaking of a switch in allegiance to a particular creed or belief, but of a transformed vision of the cosmos and one's role in it as a spiritual being.

Several other traditions pend from or fill out the initiatory importance of the central Cosmic Cross. In some early commentaries, for instance, baptism is explicitly linked both to the Cross of Christ (and thus Golgotha) and to his burial (and thus the Sepulcher): "Baptism is a cross." writes John Chrysostom, "What the Cross was to Christ and what His burial was, that baptism was to us."[24] And Ambrose says that when baptism occurs "you take on the likeness of death and burial; you receive the sacrament of the Cross."[24] It is not really surprising that references to these two primary nodes should appear in connection with the rites of initiation. For the initiatory experience is always in some form a return to the Source, a death and rebirth occurring at the Center of creation and existence.

Golgotha and the Holy Sepulcher are also particularly linked to the figure of Joseph of Arimethea. In the New Testament, the body of Christ is given into Joseph's care to be properly prepared for burial in the tomb.

Later apocryphal works provide additional details. The fourth century *Gospel of Nicodemus* holds a place of special importance in the development of the traditions. It relates how Joseph, having been imprisoned in a windowless room for his central role in the burial of Christ, is miraculously released at the very moment of the Resurrection. Some versions have Joseph later being bricked into a massive wall for teaching the Gospel. He is discovered years after, alive and unharmed, having been sustained by light and food from heaven.[2]

These and other traditions† garnered from this apocryphal gospel and its variants, form the basis for much of Robert de Boron's *Roman de l'Estoire dou Graal*. Probably composed at the end of the twelfth century, this great synthesis of Esoteric Traditions focuses on the relation of Joseph of Arimethea to the Holy Grail— the latter being a symbol of the Center *par excellence*. It tells how Joseph uses the cup of the Last Supper to catch the blood that flowed from Christ's wounds at the Crucifixion. He hides the cup and is later imprisoned. There Christ appears to him and gives him the same cup to sustain him for the time he will remain in prison. When Joseph asks what he has done to deserve such a gift, Christ responds "Thou didst take me down from the Cross and lay me in thy sepulchre..."[57,90]

Joseph of Arimethea bearing the Body of Christ - Chartres.

Joseph becomes the Grail Bearer precisely because he is intimately connected to the Cosmic Mysteries of the Cross and the Tomb.

According to other legends Joseph of Arimethea traveled to Glastonbury, England, bearing with him the vessel of the Grail. It is said that when he arrived he stuck his staff into the top of a hill and lay down to rest. When he awoke, the staff had rooted. This grew into a tree which burst into flower every year on Christmas day. In our chapter on the Axis we saw how the staff of the wood of the Tree of Life flowered for another Joseph—the Carpenter. We noted then that the staff was a symbol of the World Axis. A similar interpretation applies here, emphasized in the threefold configuration of staff, tree, and hill or mountain. Moreover, the very fact that the bearer of the staff and the Grail had a leading role in the events surrounding the Crucifixion reminds us of the close links among Axis, Cross, Center, and Holy Sepulcher.

†Most notably, Christ's Descent to the Underworld and the story of Seth's search for the Oil of Mercy.

The Holy Grail takes many forms including stone, tomb, head, platter, cruet, and chalice. A powerful symbol of the Center, the Grail is intimately connected to the processes of transformation and regeneration. Shown here as a chalice at the foot of the Cross, it designates the energies of cosmic regeneration that were released both at the moment of the Crucifixion and, through the symbolic link of the chalice with the Tomb of Christ, at the time of the Resurrection.

At one point in de Boron's *Graal*, Jesus tells Joseph that in the future "tables" (or altars) will be set up, then says:

> The table signifies the Cross; the vessels in which the sacrifice and consecration will be made signify the grave wherein thou didst lay me. This is the cup in which my body will be consecrated in the form of the Host. The paten that will be laid upon it signifies the stone with which thou didst close the mouth of the tomb, the cloth that will be spread over it signifies the linen that thou woundest round my body.[57,90] †

†We find the same esoteric symbolism in a work of Honorius of Auton on the Liturgy. He writes "When the priest says *per omnia saecula saeculorum,* the deacon comes before him and elevates the chalice. He covers a portion of it with a cloth, then returns it to the altar and covers it with the corporal, enacting the part of Joseph of Arimethea who took the body of Christ down from the cross, covered his face with a sudarium, laid the body in the grave and covered it with a stone. That which is here offered , and also the chalice, are covered with the corporeal, which signifies the linen winding sheet in which Joseph wrapped the body of Christ. The Chalice signifies the grave, and the paten the stone with which it was closed."[57] The symbolism goes back much further than this, however, at least to fourth century Syria. *The Homilies* of Theodore of Mopsuestia say that "it is in a sort of tomb that Christ is placed on the altar.. That is why some of the deacons, who lay out the cloths on the altar, show by this action the likeness of the burial cloths.." [21]

This symbolism is linked to what de Boron calls "The Great Sacrament of the Grail," really a kind of cosmic Mass. The energies involved in the events of the Crucifixion, Descent to the Underworld, and Resurrection are invoked each time the ceremony is performed. The Created Order symbolized by the Cross and Table/Altar is the stage for this spiritual activity.

We are dealing with a truing, or redemption of the cosmos. The theme is elaborated upon in de Boron's later description of the table set up by Joseph and of the ceremony performed there: When the land becomes barren, Joseph prays for help before the vessel of the Holy Grail. He is instructed to set up a table and to place the grail vessel at its center. Of those who come to participate in the ceremony only the pure in heart are able to approach the table and receive the grace of the Grail. The land is restored when those who cannot perceive the power of the Grail leave the community. In other words, the regeneration of the cosmos requires the mediative efforts of those who have placed themselves in correct relation to the Center .

Allied to this theme we have again the doctrine of the interdependency of macrocosm and microcosm, a perception of the great chain of being linking the universe and its denizens. Because of their awareness of this inherent synergy between Creator, Cosmos and Man, ancient writers, artists and builders attempted to replicate, in symbolic fashion, the image of a perfected universe—incorporating, wherever possible, cosmic correspondences into their work.

As far as Christianity is concerned such correspondences are particularly evident in the layout of its sacred buildings. A striking example relevant to our current discussion is found in a passage from Procopius of Gaza (ca 540). He describes the plan of a church in Constantinople:

> The lines were drawn in the form of a cross, joining one another in the middle, the upright one pointing to the rising and the setting sun, and the other cross line towards the north and south wind. These were surrounded by a circuit of walls, and within by columns placed both above and below; at the crossing of the two straight lines, that is, about the middle

This 14th century drawing shows the plan of a Church
overlaid on the human form.

point of them, there is a place set apart that may not be entered except by the priests, and which is consequently termed
the sanctuary.[64]

Here the whole building is aligned with natural forces—the
course of the sun and the winds. Furthermore, since this church
(like most sacred edifices) incorporates the symbolism of the
cross, it mirrors the spiritual structure of the universe. On one
level, we have an image of the Mystical Body of Christ laid upon
the Cosmic Cross. On another level, we have a likeness of the
human body. Durandus of Mende *(ca 1100)* states explicitly: "The
form of the church corresponds to the parts of the human body."[97]
Peter of Celle *(1187)* calls the nave of a church a "belly" or
"womb" *(venter)*, and the chevet he calls the "head" *(caput)*.[97]
Maximus the Confessor *(580-662)*, remarks that the church is a

Christ with the Gifts of the Spirit in the
form of a six-pointed cross radiating from
his heart - St. Denis, France.

figure of God, an image of the world "composed of visible and invisible substances," and a likeness of the human being—body, soul and spirit.[68] Included in the symbolism of the church (or at least certain churches) is the entire complex of subtle psychic and spiritual energies that underpin physical human existence. In short, the church is a reflection of the total human being, just as it is a mirror of the whole of the cosmos. At the center of all is the Sacred Heart. Represented in the church by the sanctuary and the altar, it is at once the Heart of God, the Cosmic Center, and the heart/center of the human being.

In addition to being the esoteric basis for the design of ancient churches, the three dimensional Cosmic Cross flowing forth from the Sacred Center provides the essential model for the Theurgic rites of mediation. This is an important point. Since most modern Christian Adepts are anonymous, independent clergy, they generally have little opportunity to *openly* exercise their gifts and traditions within an actual physical church of the right layout and proportion. Although some Magi known to us have special house-based chapels (as in the early days of Christianity) most improvise space as best they can, relying upon an inner or ritual model of the Cross to link to the Center—to the Point where "the power of God, flowing together from the four quarters, stands still."

The exercise below (and the one which follows the next chapter) is based in part upon just such a model.

Exercise:
THE SUN CHALICE

Start with *the Kenotic Opening*, then recite the phrase for *the Sphere of Creation*, becoming aware of a sphere of light building around you, its boundaries coinciding with the boundaries of your aura.

The sphere expands. As it grows, its light separates into innumerable points that flash as stars upon a backdrop of indigo darkness.

Recite the phrase for *the Lance of Light* and become aware of the axis of light running through the poles of the cosmic sphere and through the line of your spinal column.

Now chant the phrase for *The Living Flame.* You are conscious of a stream of golden fire descending along the line of the axis. It passes though your spinal column and descends to the center of the earth, kindling there a secret fire. The stream of fire rises, entering the base of your spine and rushes up to your head, before it fades into a single golden flame in your heart.

Look into the center of the flame. Its golden radiance grows, becoming so bright that you feel as if the sun itself were rising within you.

Out of this brightness, you perceive patches of color. These sharpen into a landscape, similar to the landscape of your previous visions, but now transfigured into a likeness of the earthly paradise.

You stand upon the world mountain. Immediately before you rises a great cosmic tree, its heaven spread branches filled with flaming leaves and luminous fruit. These, you realize, correspond with the cosmic planes and levels of being. You are aware also, in translucent vision, of the roots of the tree spreading throughout the mountain, deep into the earth, touching upon a series of wondrous crystal caves. Here lie the mighty elemental forces that shape the world, and you acknowledge them with a ritual gesture of respect.

Near the base of the tree you see a huge glowing emerald, its surface carved with arcane symbols. From a cleft in this sacred stone springs the source of the four world rivers.

You look at the magical landscape around you and marvel at the redolent verdure and life which emanates from every detail. You are aware of many animals in the landscape, not only the more familiar birds and beasts of the world but also mythical creatures like the unicorn and the phoenix. You are conscious also of a great host of elemental and angelic beings, including the guardians of this hidden realm, by whose leave you have entered here, and whose very presence seems to sound a chorus to the ineffable beauty of this secret place.

And you become aware of the companionship of inner plane adepti, and among them mysterious presences of deep spiritual authority—Masters, Saints, and Magi—who instill within you a profound sense of peace.

You are drawn to gaze again upon the emerald stone. As you do so you are aware of a shift in your consciousness and you feel a strengthening within you of the link between the realm of imaginal symbols and the world of pure spirit.

You see a great mandorla appear above the stone, its

outline faint at first, but quickly growing into an almond of golden light. As you look into this light, you see, translucently silhouetted within it, a mighty figure of the Cosmic Christ, royal, crowned and robed, his palms pressed together before his heart in the familiar position of prayer.

He looks down upon the assembled company, then stretches out his arms in a gesture of blessing. As his hands part before him, a six-pointed cross of light bursts forth from his heart, raying out to the height and depth and length and breadth of the cosmos, offering a blessing of love, power and wisdom to the entire created order in all its visible and invisible aspects.

And now there comes from within the central point of the cross, a rush of radiance. You are enveloped by an immeasurable illumination. You realize that in some mysterious way your being has been touched by the Source of all being.

The light fades, and with it fades the paradisal vision, leaving you once again conscious of yourself at the center of the star-covered cosmic sphere. The sphere contracts, drawing the stars together into one sphere of pure star light. You are aware also of the lance of light running through your spinal column and through the poles of the aura sized sphere which now encompasses you.

And deep within your heart is the spark of golden fire. Out of the root of this flame, fine lines of bright golden-white light, like the rays of the sun, shoot up weaving themselves into the form of a cup, a veritable sun chalice. You meditate upon the meaning of this symbol at the center of your being, reciting, as you do so, the selected ritual phrase (*suggestions*: "A chalice in the sacred heart;" "Blessed are those who seek the Grail;" "Be hallowed by a holy grail.").

v

the
wheel of life

The Wheel of Life is a practical Esoteric Key based on a primordial fourfold and/or sevenfold division of time and space. Based, that is, on the fourfold seasonal cycle of spring, summer, fall and winter; the cycle of the day as expressed in the points of dawn, midday, dusk, and midnight; the lunar cycle; the rotational rising and setting of the stars; and on the four cardinal directions of East, South, West, and North. In sevenfold form these cycles and divisions combine with linear or axial models of time and space: past, present, future; and below, center, above.

However configured, the patterns of sacred time and space always have biological, psychic, and spiritual harmonics within creation. Indeed, according to esoteric teaching the patterns of creation are themselves "mirrors" of Divinity. And it is no surprise that we find in the early strata of Christian Tradition a fair number of references to this reflective or symbolic property of the cosmos. In the third century, for instance, Cyprian of Carthage wrote:

> It is in imitation of the Lord himself that the sun completes the 365 days of the year and the fourfold division of the day. Now each of these four divisions of the day has three hours in it. And three of the hours carry the image of those three days that in the beginning of time were without sun or moon. Likewise those three (primordial) days were revealed

in the adding of three hours four times over four years to produce one (extra) day of twelve hours; and in the four seasons of three months each; and in the twelve month course of the year. Thus, through multiform threefoldness, the twelve hours have been displayed in the four divisions of the one Gospel. And the three months in the course of (each of) the four seasons, that is in the course of the four Gospels, have revealed to us the Twelve Apostles chosen by Christ. [77]

In this passage, Cyprian presents the essentials of a model of sacred time. He begins by designating the annual and diurnal cycles of the Sun as *imitationes Christi*. He then develops the idea, correlating the primordial creation with the cycle of the day. In accordance with the ancient sundial, a cycle of twelve hours is given, with one quarter of these in darkness. These three hours of darkness (=6 hours in modern time) resonate with the three days of darkness before the creation of the sun and moon at the beginning of time (see *Genesis 1*). The same primordial processes are repeated or reflected in the year of four seasons and twelve months. Fused with this temporal structure are the patterns of the Four Gospels and the Twelve Apostles— the twelve hours of the fourfold day and the twelve months of the fourfold year are analogous to the Twelve Apostles of the Four Gospels.

Just as Cyprian's work places the Four Gospels in relation to sacred time, so do other authors relate these holy stories to the shape of sacred space. The second century bishop, Irenaeus,† for example, remarks upon their accordance with the structure of the cosmos as follows:

The Gospels could not be either greater or lesser in number than they are. For since there are four regions of the world

---

†Because of his vehement polemic towards certain "Gnostic" sects, Irenaeus is generally dismissed as a despiser of all things esoteric. This view, however, is inaccurate. Irenaeus' truculence stems not from his dislike of esoteric tradition, but from his desire to protect or preserve what he considered the true esoteric teachings from corruption by certain creation negating influences current within some of the Gnostic systems of the Second Century. Read with discretion, Ireneaus' works yield many gems of esoteric wisdom.

Dome in St. Mark's, Venice, showing the Four Archangels and the Kerubic forms of the Four Evangelists.

This dome, at St. Zeno, shows the Four Gospels and Evangelists within the regions of the Four Quarters. At the arms of the cross, holding up the cosmic sphere, are four Magi.

The Four Archangels consecrating a church. Clockwise from top right are Raphael making a sign of blessing in the air, Michael blessing with incense, Gabriel asperging with water, and Auriel blessing and sounding the church bell. From a window at Greater Malvern Priory, England.

in which we live, and four Universal Spirits, and since the Church is disseminated over the whole earth, and the pillar and firmament of the Church is the Gospel and the Spirit of Life; it follows that she should have four pillars breathing forth incorruptibility in all directions and vivifying people everywhere.[71]

For Irenaeus, there are four Gospels precisely because there are four regions or quarters to the world. Irenaeus goes on to comment upon the Four Kerubic Creatures† ascribed to the Four Evangelists and Gospels: Lion, Ox, Eagle, Man. On the one hand, he remarks, each animal/Gospel symbolizes four "dispensations" of Christ through the ages as Logos, Praxis ("a priestly and liturgical practice"), Cosmic Spirit (literally "the Celestial Spirit over all the Earth"), and Man. On the other hand the Kerubic images correspond with four ages or epochs: the Adamic Age, the Age of Noah, the Age of Moses, and the Fourth Age (of the Christos or, perhaps, of Mary) which "renovates man and reca-

†Which, as he remarks, derive from Ezekiel's vision of the Tetramorphs *(Ez. 10:14)*.

pitulates all within itself through the (fourfold) Gospel."

Of particular interest also is Irenaeus' mention of the Four Universal Spirits associated with the four quarters. These are likely the Four Archangels Raphael, Michael, Gabriel and Auriel. Although the first three names are still familiar to many people, the name of the fourth Archangel, Auriel, or Uriel, is not well known. In point of fact, however, the four were closely allied in ancient times. The Four Archangels are mentioned individually in certain books of the Bible and Apocrypha.† They appear to-

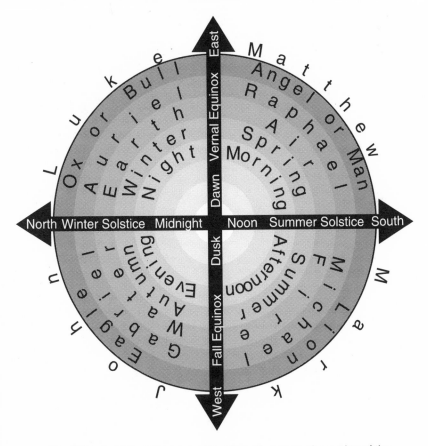

The Wheel of Life. The cross of the four directions, the cycles of the day and seasons, and the Elements and beings of the Quarters.

†Raphael in the *Book of Tobit*; Gabriel in *Daniel* & *Luke*; Michael in *Daniel*, *Jude* and *Revelation*; Uriel in *2 Esdras*.

gether in the esoteric *Epistle of the Apostles* (2nd century) where they are said to have accompanied Christ into the fifth sphere of the heavens. Isidore of Seville (560-636) also mentions the four by name and outlines their attributes. The fact that the conventional Church banned the veneration of Uriel at the Council of Rome in 745 also suggests the Archangel played a role of some significance in the folk-magical traditions of Europe.

The Archangels may be seen as four great Guardian beings, as stewards or caretakers of creation with special relationships to cosmic cycles and structures. They are generally assigned to the four directions as follows: Raphael in the East, Michael in the South, Gabriel in the West, and Auriel in the North. The names of the Archangels also suggest aspects of their spiritual role in creation: Raphael, "healer of God," has much to do with healing and guiding energies. Michael, "likeness of God," is on one level concerned with enabling the interchange of spiritual power between the worlds, and on another with high mystical experiences of an apocalyptic type where consciousness of all worlds and planes passes away as the soul joins in direct union with Ultimate Being. Gabriel, "power or strength of God," has to do with creative and purifying energies. Auriel, "light or radiance of God," has to do with the mediation of the inner light of wisdom to the outer world.

This diagram from the 12th century shows Man, the Microcosm, surrounded by the Four Elements: Among other things, Air relates to breath and perceptions; Water to blood, Earth to flesh and bones, Fire to bodily warmth and the vital spirit.
The nimbus contains the rays of the seven planets. Clockwise from the left these are: Saturn, Mars, Jupiter, Sun, Moon, Mercury, and Venus - *Hortus Deliciarum.*

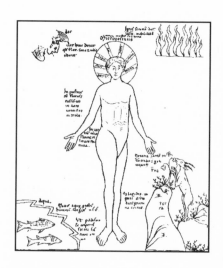

We might add to our quaternal model of cosmic energies the attributes of the Four Elements. Methodius of Olympus (ca. 312 A.D.), for example, links the Elements to the Kerubic Creatures as follows: The Man or Angel corresponds to Air, the Ox to Earth, the Lion to Fire, and the Eagle to Water. "God, then,....holding air and earth, water and fire in his hand and ruling them by his will, like a four-horsed chariot, in an unutterable way controls the universe and keeps it in being."[72, 20] The Four Elements characterize the "psychic substance" of the universe. They express certain energies or principles of creation—principles which are naturally reflected in the soul and life of man. Very briefly: Air is the element of activity, light, clarity, abstraction, impulse and repulse, and corresponds to the mental nature. Fire symbolizes growth, life, illumination, consummation, transformation, the desire nature. Water cleanses, forms, purifies, fills and empties; it is depth, and love, the emotional nature. Earth is concerned with the energies of solidity, of patterning, steadfastness, law, shaping and transforming through pressure, the physical nature.

Where this concern with fourfold symbolism is leading is to the recognition or recovery of a great system of correspondences based upon the Mystery of the Cosmic Cross. As we saw in our last chapter the Cosmic Cross represents the underlying unified spiritual structure of the universe—a structure ultimately identified with the mystical body of Christ. There is a Coptic apocryphal gospel which tells how at the birth of Christ a star appears in the form of a wheel, its figure like a cross— in other words a circled cross. On the cross are emblazoned the words "This is Jesus the Son of God." This image of star-wheel or circled cross expresses at least two levels of significance. On one hand, the image fulfills a conventional function as a sign pointing to the place where the Christ Child is born. On the other hand, the image is itself a symbol of the Christ nature. In the latter case, the words "This is Jesus the Son of God" refer to the mysteries of the Cosmic Christ as expressed through the universal symbolism of the circled cross. Irenaeus also writes on the theme of the Cosmic Christ:

> Now seeing that he is the Logos of God Almighty, who in unseen wise in our midst is universally extended in all the

world, and encompasses its length and breadth and height and depth—for by the Logos of God the whole universe is ordered and disposed—in it is crucified the Son of God, inscribed crosswise upon it all: for it is right that he, being made visible, should set upon all things visible the sharing of his Cross, that he might show his operation on visible things through a visible form. For he it is who illuminates the height that is the heavens; and encompasses the deep that is beneath the earth; and stretches and spreads out the length from east to west; and steers across the breadth of north and south; summoning all that are scattered in every quarter to the knowledge of the Father.[52]

Once again the Bishop of Lyon is concerned primarily with sacred space. Here, however, the horizontal plane of the four directions has developed a central vertical axis—the cosmic circled cross expressed in three dimensions. We have met with this figure of the three-dimensional cross before, in particular, in a passage from the *Clementine Homilies* where it was shown to be the primordial pattern underlying the manifestation of sacred event, space, and time. Sacred space not only has a hori-

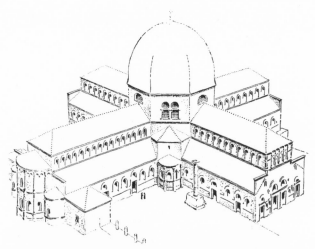

Domed, cruciform Church of St. Simon Stylites
at Kal'at Sim'ân, Syria - circa 450 AD. Note the four naves
obviously designed for use at the four seasons.

zontal polarity of length and breadth expressed as regions, quarters, directions, but a vertical polarity of celestial realm and underworld—all arrayed round a central primordial point. Time may also be said to have a horizontal plane manifested through the cosmic cycles of sun, moon and stars (as in the seasons, day, months, and zodiac) and a linear or vertical axis running from the past, through the eternal present and into the future. Properly speaking, we are dealing with a flow of energies which are neither cyclic nor linear, but spiral. The pattern forms the basis for the structure and action of ritual, the design of the church, temple, or ritual area, and, of course, the ritual calendar.

As symbolic glyphs built upon the general pattern of the Wheel of Life, all sacred calendars are primordial, perennial and universal. In terms of their precise details, however, there is considerable fluidity involved. In the following discussion we have not deemed it necessary to adhere to any rigid designation of dates. We have, however, tried to strike a balance between tradition, esoteric teaching, and intuitive perception. Our concerns are not with the nostalgic commemoration or celebration of "historical" events or activities *per se*. We are here primarily interested in the magical and initiatory aspects of the sacred calendar.

There are two main components to the sacred calendar of Magical Christianity. The more important of the two we term the *Christological Cycle*, and the other the *Sanctoral Cycle*. The former deals with the Magical Life of Christ, the latter with the esoteric significance of the legendary acts of the apostles, saints, and angels.

Looking at the overall pattern of the Christological Cycle we note that all the main events take place roughly within one half of the year with a high concentration near the winter solstice and the spring equinox (see Figure A). This dispersement near the focal points of solstice and equinox gives a cosmic emphasis to the experiences of resurrection, rebirth, and regeneration which lie at the heart of the Magical Christian Tradition. For both these points have to do with the seasonal increase of light and cosmic energy in the world. The winter solstice marks the juncture in the year when the days begin to progressively lengthen. The spring equinox heralds the beginning of days that are longer than the nights.

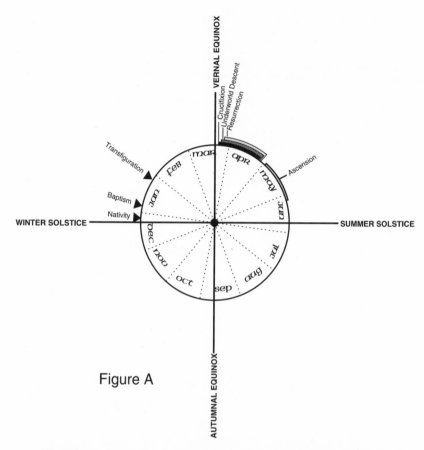

Figure A

The Wheel of Life showing the pattern of the Christological Cycle. A variation on the pattern would attribute the Nativity to the winter solstice, the Baptism to the first new moon after the solstice, and the Transfiguration to the following full moon.

There are great psychic tides associated with the solstices and equinoxes. The entire year is encompassed by an overlapping ebb and flow of cosmic energies. These surges of energy can be tapped through ritual and meditation and are a great store of inner power for the adepti of all Esoteric Traditions.

The energies released at the solstices and equinoxes are mirrored in the rotational pattern of the four seasons. These in turn resonate with the fourfold cycle of the day and with the lunar cycle. The round of the cosmic tides also finds its reflection in the human life cycle and in the patterns of human activity. For all has its rise, apogee, decline and fall. It might be useful to briefly tabulate some of the processes involved in the fourfold cosmic cycle. Meditation upon the following list of keywords will deepen one's understanding of these cyclic energies:

The Christological component of the esoteric calendar has to do, as we have said, with the Magical Life of Christ. In this,

Solstice	Equinox	Solstice	Equinox
Winter	Spring	Summer	Autumn
Storing	Sowing	Tending	Harvesting
Gestating	Germinating	Flowering	Wilting
Inbreathing	Inbreathing	Outbreathing	Outbreathing
Midnight	Dawn	Noon	Dusk
Night	Morning	Afternoon	Evening
Nadir	Ascent	Apogee	Descent
Set	Arising	Risen	Descending
Originating	Developing	Establishing	Completing
Birth	Youth	Maturity	Death
Afterlife	Birth	Life	Death
New	Waxing	Full	Waning
Empty	Filling	Full	Emptying
Low	Flow	High	Ebb

there are seven key initiations or Mysteries. These have much to do with the ongoing release of regenerative spiritual energies throughout the Three Worlds and the Planes of Being. The archetypal pattern of the Christ life provides an exemplary model for certain types of inner experience and mediatory or theurgic practice. There is space here to deal only with the major images, and these in brief, but this should more than suffice to show the importance of the pattern as a whole.

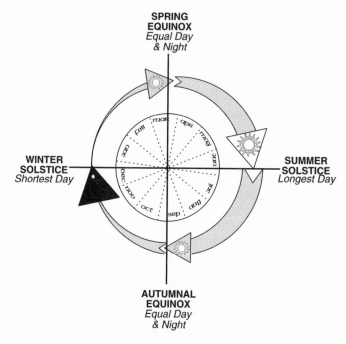

The Wheel of Life showing the rise and fall of the solar light through
the course of the year

THE NATIVITY *(December 25)*:

At one time, the Nativity was celebrated as part of the
Epiphany on January 6th or 7th. It was moved, in the fourth
century, to the 25th of December in order to have it coincide
with the Roman feast of *Sol Invictus*, a celebration of the birth
of the Unconquered Sun. Originally the Nativity may have been
a movable feast like Easter, because we are obviously concerned
with the winter solstice, which occurs between the 21st and 23rd
of December each year. The winter solstice is the point at which
the days, having reached their shortest duration, now begin to
lengthen. Symbolically light wins out over darkness. More than
this however, we must consider that at the solstice, the energies
of the earth are most indrawn. The plant and animal life is contained within the earth to its fullest extent. The angelic and
elemental powers connected with vegetation and growth are also
withdrawn into the earth. It is at this moment, the moment

The Birth of Christ in a cave.

when the earth is most fecund, most pregnant with cosmic energy, that the Divine Child is born in the depths of a cave.

The Christ Child is closely tied to the very structure of nature. One might say the Child manifests at the center of nature. According to one legend, at the birth of the Christ Child "the sun in the east bowed down, the stars stood still, the mountains and the forests shook and touched the earth with their summits and the heaven and earth were bowed."

Further, we know from the legends and from the timing of Christmas and Epiphany† that the Divine Child is intimately linked with the cycles of the sun and moon. These two repre-

†At one time, the Epiphany was likely celebrated on the first new moon after the winter solstice.

117

sent polarity, male and female, active and receptive, and so on. In fact, contained within the bipolar symbolism of the sun and moon as linked to the Christ Child we have a definite remnant of at least a part of the original intent of Christianity. Namely, that it was to present a balanced alternative to the severely patriarchal religion of the Old Testament. There was originally an attempt to balance the male and female energies of the soul. Had it not been for certain so-called "Pauline" influences within the political Church more elements of this balance may well have been retained. Nonetheless, it is interesting to note here that as a symbol the Child is an androgynous being, balancing male and female, unifying the sun and the moon.

We are beginning to get a picture of the function and significance of the birth of the Christ Child as an archetypal event. We might summarize this picture as follows:

1) The Divine Child unifies opposites.

2) The Christ Child represents a center, both of our own personal being, and by extension of the collective being, of nature, and of the planetary being. Another way of putting this is to say that the Christ Child is the spiritual Center of the cosmos.

It should be reasonably apparent that the symbolic significance of the Holy Child meshes with the meaning, and inner structure of the Christmas period to form a coherent whole, all of which must be taken into account when we speak of the inner meaning of the Nativity.

THE BAPTISM *(January 6)*:

As a cosmic event the Baptism of Christ involves the drawing together, fusion, and release into the terrestrial world of celestial and underworld forces. The latter are symbolized by the elements of fire and water respectively—fire representing the power of the spirit and water the principle of primordial potency. Referring to Christ's Baptism, Clement of Alexandria writes "The new creation comes about by water and the spirit, like the creation of the universe: The spirit of God was borne upon the waters."[21]

According to art and legend, when Jesus descended into the

Jordan it was enflamed, and when he rose from it the water also rose seething around him. There is an ancient tradition cited by Cyril of Jerusalem in the fourth century that the river Jordan issued forth from the mouth of a dragon. The river is thus the dragon's breath, the cosmic *kundalini* which is lifted up and consecrated by the Christ being. At the same time, according to some traditions, the spirit descends from above in the form of a fiery dove.

The resulting fusion of the energies of above and below and their dispersal or mediation into the terrestrial realm transforms the world by drawing it into closer configuration with its prototype. As Gregory of Nyssa writes in his *de baptismo*, after Christ's Baptism the Jordan enveloped the entire world, and following along the channels of the four rivers which flow out from the earthly paradise "carried back into paradise things far more precious than those which came out."[21] This is the irradiation of the great cosmic dragon force. Now "christified" or consecrated, it transfigures the entire world, by transforming its paradisal prototype. Through the Mystery of the Baptism the earthly paradise is reconfigured to the pattern of a new creation.

THE TRANSFIGURATION *(January 20)*:

The Transfiguration complements the Mystery of the Nativity. For while the Birth occurs in the context of underworld symbolism (Christ is born amidst the creational energies in the depths of the womb of the earth mother, also in darkness, in a cave, etc.,.), the Transfiguration takes place on a mountain, that is within the context of the celestial or overworld powers. The mountain where Christ's Transfiguration occurred is traditionally said to have been Mt. Tabor, which derives from *tabbur* meaning "navel." In other words, the Tranfiguration occurs at the Center, on the World Mountain. In sacred lore, the ascent of the World Mountain is always an ascent through the heavens and planes of being. At the peak is the dark cloud—a symbol of the unfathomable divinity of non-being, or uncreate reality.

On a cosmic level, the Mystery of the Transfiguration involves a rupture or breach of the planes bringing the divine reality into direct contact with the physical and psychic planes. This opening of a gateway between the worlds also enables contact with the higher orders of Adepti, Saints, and Masters which in the tradition of the Transfiguration are represented by the figures of Moses and Elija.

Moreover, Christ takes several of his initiates with him to the mountain where to a degree they participate in the Transfiguration. The Transfiguration thus provides a model for "deification," for the enlightenment or illumination of the initiate.

The Transfiguration.

As Gregory Palamas writes "[T]he deifying gift of the Spirit is a mysterious light, and transforms into light those who receive its richness."[43] And elsewhere in the same work the author remarks how some of the saints "have seen this light as a limitless sea, flowing forth in a paradoxical manner from the unique Sun, that is, from the adorable Body of Christ, as in the case of the apostles on the Mountain. It is thus that the first fruits of our human constitution are deified."[43] Because of this connection to the Body of Christ, the Transfiguration is also especially linked with the ritual pattern of Holy Communion.

THE CRUCIFIXION *(three days prior to the Resurrection)*:

We have mentioned several times in this book the significance of the three dimensional cross as an extension or creational development of the cosmic Center. The cross is the great symbol both of cosmic unity, and of the realignment of the cosmic order. The world is redeemed because it is fused with the divine being who is, in the words of Irenaeus, "inscribed crosswise upon it all." Maximus the Confessor speaks of the Crucified Christ as "he who encloses in himself all beings....As the center of straight lines that radiate from him he does not allow by his unique, simple, and single cause and power that the principles of beings become disjoined at the periphery, but rather he circumscribes their extension in a circle (or sphere) and brings back to himself the distinctive elements of beings who he brought into existence."[68] The Crucifixion of Christ on one level, then, is nothing less than his mergence with the universe and all who live and move and have their being therein:

> I am the light that is over all things.
> I am all:
>> all came forth from me,
>> and all attained to me.
> Split a piece of wood,
>> and I am there.
> Pick up a stone,
>> and you will find me there.
> (*Gospel of Thomas,* Logion 75)[95]

It is the promise of this universal vision which places the Crucifixion as an initiatory image in certain Magical Christian rituals. These rites involve opening the soul to an awareness of the immeasurable workings of divinity within the cosmos. During the experience the individual ego "dies" to itself and is reconfigured to the higher self. This is one reason initiation earns the epithet "living death." There is a realignment of the human soul, a redemption, resurrection, or reattunment to a primordial spiritual vision. The life energy of the initiate is no longer primarily focused on personal development or enlightenment, but turns now to matters of cosmic mediation.

THE DESCENT TO THE UNDERWORLD *(three days between Crucifixion and Resurrection):*

On a cosmic level, the Descent to the Underworld involves the emptying, restructuring and realignment of the energies of the underworld. According to ancient traditions,† through Christ's Descent the underworld is emptied, souls are freed, "the abysses are opened and closed," death is conquered. The underworld is reconfigured according to the cosmic pattern of the cross (Christ sets up a cross of light in the underworld —*Gospel of Nicodemus*). Moreover the primal man, Adam, is restored to paradise and the way to the Tree of Life, that is to the powers of the Universal Axis, is reopened.

These transformations in the underworld structure make certain initiatory experiences available to the individual soul. The way to "paradise" is eased: The unconscious or hidden reaches of the soul are emptied of their "infernal" or "demonic" elements, easing passage through the underworld reaches. John Chrysostom says that into the darkness of the underworld "the sun of Righteousness descended and lightened it, making Heaven of Hades."[66] In esoteric traditions, "paradise" is reached by traveling through the underworld.

The Descent to the Underworld involves the reattunment of those underworld forces which shape the world as we know it. In one sense, the underworld is restored to its primal form—the

---

†The Descent, though not specifically mentioned in the conventional Gospels, is at least alluded to in *Matthew 13*, and it has an important place in many Apocryphal works, the most important being the *Gospel of Nicodemus*.

fecund cosmic womb, the place of spiritual rebirth and re-creation, the point of Resurrection.

THE RESURRECTION (*first full moon after spring equinox*):

In canto xxiii of the *Paradiso,* Dante has a vision of the "shining substance" of the Risen Christ. The vision takes place in the eighth sphere of the heavens, that is, the region of the zodiac and the fixed stars. Dante's vision accords with early traditions that speak of Christ's Resurrection as occurring on the "eighth day." In ancient cosmology the seven days of the week correspond to the seven planetary spheres of the visible heavens. An "eighth day," according to this reckoning, would represent the eighth celestial sphere, that is, the *ogdoad* or sphere of the fixed stars. This symbolism of the Mystery of the Resurrection suggests at once both the incarnation within the earthly sphere of the primordial, perfect, "zodiacal man," and the raising up of the physical plane itself to the level of the archetypes. In one sense, Christ's Resurrection Body is of an archetypal "stellar" or "sidereal" nature with the power to utterly regenerate the cosmos. In speaking of the reason why spring is the most appropriate time for the Resurrection, Eusebius remarks "this time was the very one which appeared at the moment of the first creation of the world, when the earth brought forth shoots and the stars appeared; it is at this time

The Resurrection.

that the Lord of the whole world celebrated the mystery of his own feast and, like a great star, appeared to light up the whole world...and thus to bring back the anniversary of the cosmos."[21]

The Resurrected Christ giving the secret teaching to the Apostles-Chartres.

Another reason the Resurrection is linked closely to springtime is because the vernal equinox marks the moment from which daylight begins to outlast night. Light becomes the predominant force in the world, and hence it is now that the teachings of light are traditionally given out to the Apostles. The period following the Resurrection constitutes a higher octave of the time which followed the Baptism of Christ, when Jesus first began his mission as teacher and healer. This is why nearly all of the esoteric apocryphal works claim to present a hidden teaching or gnosis received directly from the Risen Christ (e.g. *Gospel of Thomas, Acts of John, Acts of Peter, Apocryphal Gospel of John*, etc.):

Let me disclose all secrets;
Let me reveal the forms of all gods;
And the hidden mystery of the Way
Called Gnosis, let me impart.
(Hymn quoted by Hippolytus)[66]

THE ASCENSION *(forty days after the Resurrection)*:

Certain of the teachings ascribed to the Risen Christ concern knowledge of the spiritual structure of the cosmos (i.e. the nature of the various planes and heavens), the mysteries of Christ's descent and ascent through the cosmic spheres, and instruction regarding the passage of the soul through the celestial spheres.

On one level, Christ's Ascension completes a cosmic "circuit" of spiritual force. Early legends, for instance, mention Christ descending through the seven spheres at the Incarnation. As he descends, he takes on a different form according to the nature of each sphere and thus remains unrecognized by its denizens. The work of the Incarnation takes place *incognito*, the transformation of the cosmos being wrought from within. Then in completion of the mission, Christ reascends through the planes— this time openly and in full glory. The work of the Ascension thus completes the pattern of the christification of the cosmos. The Three Worlds are infused with the Christ force. The Logos has become the nucleus of the whole created order.

But the Ascent does not "end" at the highest heaven. For while the divine being permeates and encompasses all creation, it simultaneously transcends it. One might speak then of the Ascension giving way to a "Trancension"—divine being transcending itself in the unfathomable mystery of non-being.

The pattern of the Ascension also underlies a specific *disciplinam arcani*. As "the Way," the Christ embodies the cosmic planes. This is why in some traditions he is depicted as of titanic proportions, "so large that his head reached to Heaven."[66] Participation in the Mystical Body of Christ (e.g. through the Eucharist) includes then the possibility of an experience of "rising on the planes," of passing to and fro among the realms of being, consciousness and creation.

****

The Ascent of Christ through the spheres finds a symbolic counterpoint in the descent of divine fire at Pentecost. Pentecost traditionally takes place fifty days after the Resurrection which brings it generally within the influence of the tidal energies of the summer solstice. In one sense, it can be considered as a bridge between the mysteries of the Christological Cycle and the Sanctoral Cycle. We touched upon the archetypal nature of the pentecostal experience in Chapter iii. The ability of the Apostles to speak every language marks them as representatives of all humanity. It is at this time also that the Apostles are designated different regions of the world in which to heal and

Medieval map showing the attribution of the Apostles to various lands.

teach (*Acts 2*). It is well known that long before apostolic times the various regions of the known world were associated with the signs of the zodiac. Like the lands they visited the Apostles too were linked to the twelve zodiacal signs. We have already cited traditions that correlate the Apostles with the zodiac through their association with the twelve months of the year and the ancient system of the twelve hour day.

Of additional interest is the tradition of Jesus' Round Dance. Found in the *Acts of John*, this is a ritual dance which takes place after the Last Supper. The Twelve Apostles move in a circle around the Christ, the Lord of the Dance, who sings a cosmic hymn. The hymn itself has to do with the resolution of opposites, and with a ritual lifting up of the soul enabling it to view from a cosmic perspective the rounds of birth, life, death, and rebirth, of being and non-being. In the middle of the hymn are the following lines:

The One Ogdoad sings praise with us. Amen
The Twelve dance on high. Amen.
The Whole on high joins in our dancing. Amen.
Who dances not knows not what comes to pass. Amen.[3]

Note the reference to the sphere of the stars, the *ogdoad*. The Twelve who dance on high are both the twelve signs of the zodiac and the Apostles themselves who are raised in vision to the plane of celestial archetypes. They become participants in the great dance of the cosmos. This attunement of one's being to the Wheel of Life, to the rhythms and measures of the cosmic dance, can awaken a kind of "prophetic" wisdom within the soul. One suddenly becomes aware of the great concourse and meaning of creation.

The sidereal or zodiacal aspect of the Apostles is also seen in the depictions of the Table of the Last Supper as a Round Table.

Christ and the Twelve Apostles at the Round Table of the Last Supper. After a sixth century Syrian illumination.

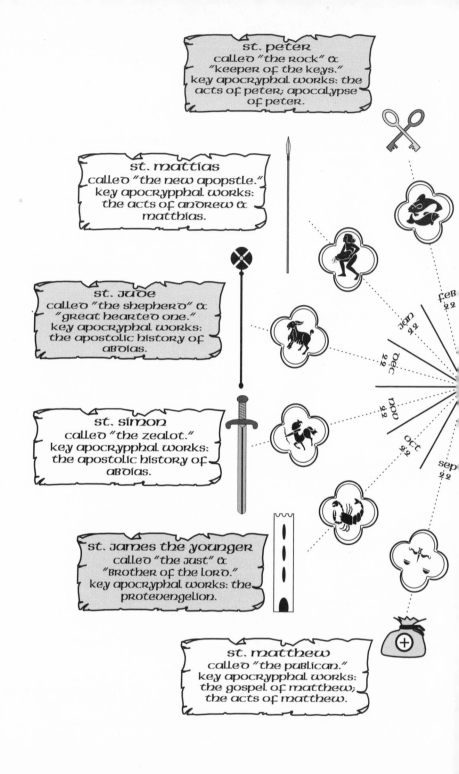

st. peter
called "the rock" &
"keeper of the keys."
key apocryphal works: the
acts of peter; apocalypse
of peter.

st. mattias
called "the new apopstle."
key apocrypphal works:
the acts of andrew &
matthias.

st. jude
called "the shepherd" &
"great hearted one."
key apocryphal works:
the apostolic history of
abdias.

st. simon
called "the zealot."
key apocrypphal works:
the apostolic history of
abdias.

st. james the younger
called "the just" &
"brother of the lord."
key apocryphal works: the
protevengelion.

st. matthew
called "the publican."
key apocrypphal works:
the gospel of matthew;
the acts of matthew.

feb 22
jan 22
dec 22
nov 22
oct 22
sep 22

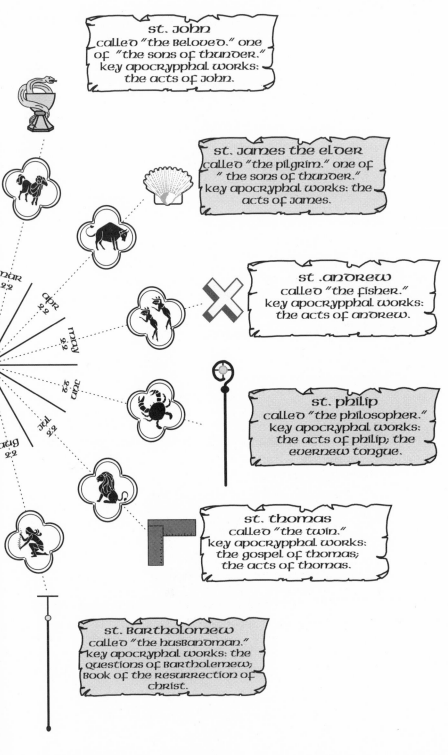

st. john
called "the beloved." one of "the sons of thunder." key apocryphal works: the acts of john.

st. james the elder
called "the pilgrim." one of "the sons of thunder." key apocryphal works: the acts of james.

st. andrew
called "the fisher." key apocryphal works: the acts of andrew.

st. philip
called "the philosopher." key apocryphal works: the acts of philip; the evernew tongue.

st. thomas
called "the twin." key apocryphal works: the gospel of thomas; the acts of thomas.

st. bartholomew
called "the husbandman." key apocryphal works: the questions of bartholomew; book of the resurrection of christ.

mar 22
apr 22
may 22
jun 22
jul 22
aug 22

The round "Agape Table" is a standard feature in many of the fourth century catacomb chapels of Malta. And in the *Queste du Saint Graal,* the Round Table set up by Merlin for the Grail Knights signifies the roundness of the cosmos, and the configurations of the planets, elements and stars.

The evidence connecting the Apostles to the zodiac, points to a secret "calendar of saints" in existence since the earliest days of Christianity. More detailed explications of the esoteric significance of the Apostles will be taken up in forthcoming works. For basic meditational, and ritual purposes, however, we give out overpage a simple chart of correspondences.

The innermost circle of the chart consists of the dates of the feasts of the Twelve Apostles. These were determined by taking the ancient Feast of the Birth of Peter as a starting point and ascribing the Apostles to successive dates at one month intervals. Rather conveniently, the Feast of the Birth of Peter (February 22) corresponds to the entry of the sun into the zodiacal sign of Pisces.† The order of the Apostles is that found in *Acts.* Although the Four Gospels give variations on this order, *Acts,* as we have said, clearly suggests zodiacal correlations. These are shown in the second circle of the chart. Beyond this are some of the symbols associated with the Twelve. Beyond this again are the names and epithets of the Apostles, along with the titles of some of the more important and accessible apocryphal works associated with them.

It will be noted that a number of the apocryphal works we have cited are Gospels, that is, they tell in some form of the acts, life, and words of Christ. There were, in early times, many more Gospels than the four which were eventually canonized by the conventional Church. Some of these apocryphal Gospels have survived in their entirety, others are now partially or entirely lost. The four traditional Gospels have a special ritual importance in Magical Christianity. For as we have seen they are symbolically linked to the cosmic cycles of nature and man. In terms of content, they also reveal, in addition to many other esoterically significant elements, the basic initiatory pattern of the Magical Life of Christ. The apocryphal Gospels fill out or

---

†The actual date of the entry of the sun into each sign varies slightly from year to year. Those with astrological knowledge can work out the exact dates for themselves.

supplement these mysteries. Taken collectively, the Gospels, *all* Gospels, constitute a great reservoir or repository of sacred lore and tradition. There is, therefore, no notion in Magical Christianity of "scriptural authority" based upon a literal or "historical" reading of the Gospels. All sacred texts, including those of Christianity, are expressions of the many-faceted archetype of the Logos. Moreover, as symbolic manifestations of the Logoic essence, all sacred texts are also incomplete. They could not be otherwise, for they attempt to express a reality greater than themselves.

In conventional Christianity the term *Logos* is normally translated as "Word." But this is somewhat misleading, and even inaccurate. *Logos* is a numinous term that includes a whole range of meaning, depending on context. Among much else it denotes

> a) a tradition, treatise, or account—which might be written, oral, or in the form of symbolic images;
> b) the principle of order or configuration;
> c) the harmonizing principle of the cosmos;†
> d) the creative principle of the cosmos.‡

It is the latter three points, in particular, which enable us to see why early writers like Irenaeus identified the Logos with the cosmic cross (or alternatively with the crucified cosmic Christ), and hence with the patterns and rhythms of the Wheel of Life. When we speak of the Four Gospels as expressions of the Logos, we are speaking, on one level, of a *theophane*—a manifestation or revelation of divine reality—appearing through the structures

†According to *The Acts of John*, the Logos is "the harmony of wisdom" and "wisdom in harmony." And in *The Acts of Peter*: "[W]hat else is Christ but the sound (i.e. harmony) of God.

‡"In the beginning was the Logos,
and the Logos was with God,
and the Logos was God.
It was in the beginning with God.
All things came into being by It,
and apart from It nothing came into being
that has come into being." *John 1:1-3*

and cycles of the cosmos. In this sense, "reading" the Gospels involves a spiritual participation in the rotation of the Life force throughout the cycles of sacred time and within the shape of sacred space. We explore this further in the exercise which follows.

Exercise:
THE SECRET GOSPELS

After the *Kenotic Opening,* proceed as usual, reciting the appropriate phrases as you build up the symbols of the previous exercises: *the Sphere of Creation, the Lance of Light, the Living Flame, and the Sun Chalice.*

You find yourself in a great stone room or chapel, with each of the four walls dominated by a tall massive, arched window filled with stained glass. In the darkened chamber you cannot clearly see the images contained within the glass.

Moving to the center of the room, you see four closed books resting on stone lecterns each facing one of the great windows. You approach the book before you, looking with awe at the finely tooled workmanship of its gold cover, richly inset with gems and jewels. You are moved to open the book. You see upon the page before you, drawn in wondrous illuminated letters, the words:

The people who sat in darkness
have seen a great light.

A gust of breeze touches your face and you look up to see the great window in front of you dissolve. You find yourself in the predawn twilight, gazing out towards the dark line of the horizon which now begins to glow pale turquoise blue. Long shadows yield to increasing light as the solar orb begins to rise. A chorus of birdsong welcomes the springtide dawn. In the distance low bushes and tall trees display their new-life green. Nearby, budding flowers begin to sway in the gentle breeze wafting their scents towards you.

Out of the light of the rising sun you see the figure of a winged man standing in the landscape. As his angelic face turns from contemplation of the dawning day towards you. You touch your hand to your heart, then raise it in salute to the mighty Kerubic creature of the East.

And now over the entire scene, you are aware of the presence of the Archangel Raphael. A titanic figure of light, robed in swirls of sun-light gold and azure blue, who holds a great and luminous crosier from the spiral of which come forth bursts of whirling wind. Amidst the spinning eddies of air is a host of luminous angelic and elemental beings. And you feel your spirit quickened by life-giving energy.

You close the golden gospel and see the window solidify, becoming a glorious scene of glass and light showing forth the figure of a winged man and beneath it, in ornate letters, the word LIGHT.

(pause for meditation)

Turning clockwise to your right you go now to the book in the South and looking upon its wonder, open it. There you see the illumined words:

To you has been given
the secret of the Kingdom.

The window fades and you become aware of the bright sun at noon. Its radiant light warms your skin and penetrates every pore of your body energizing and regenerating you. You are aware of the flowers in full bloom, the trees and bushes bearing fruit and berry, the green-ness of the grass and the richness of the land. Beneath the light of the daystar you become aware of the pres-ence of a great lion who shakes his shaggy golden mane toward the summer sun, then lowers his head to look at you. And you salute the mighty Kerubic creature of the South.   Over the entire scene is the towering presence of the Archangel Michael. See this great glo-rious being armored in red and golden light, and bear-ing a great double edged sword of fire and light. And you see a host of fiery angels and elementals streaming forth from the blazing light of the sword. You are mo-mentarily bathed in an awareness of fiery warmth and transformative light.

You close the golden gospel. The stained glass solidi-fies, disclosing in radiant, jeweled light, the image of a golden lion and beneath it, in fiery letters, the word LIFE.

(pause for meditation)

You move again to your right, that is to the Western Quarter, and open the golden book. There you see, spelled out in illuminated letters, the words:

One sows and another reaps.

The great window fades and you are aware of the quiet peace of an autumn evening. The trees are filled with leaves of red and orange and gold. The ground is covered with fruit and nuts and seed. And in the dis-tance, great fields of ripe grain sway in a gentle breeze. Immediately before you is a great river flowing strong and gracefully through the land. Looking out across the surface of the river you see, silhouetted against the orb of the setting sun, the figure of a mighty eagle, wings outspread in loving protection. Far seeing eyes turn towards you as you salute the mighty Kerubic creature of the West.

Overshadowing the entire scene is the Archangel Gabriel, a glowing figure of gigantic stature, swathed in flowing shades of deep blue and silver light, holding high a wondrous chalice of silver set with deep sapphire stones and intricately engraved with symbols. Above the rim of the chalice you see the crescent moon shining in the sky. Out of this mighty vessel, like a fount of sea foam, pours a great host of angelic and elemental beings in the colors of blue and sea green, and of silver and foamy white. You feel yourself momentarily suffused with a rich, deep encompassing love.

As you close the book the glass of the western window solidifies, glowing deeply in shades of blue to display the figure of an eagle and beneath it, in ornate silver letters, the word LOVE.

(pause for meditation)

You move to the North and open the book, seeing there the words:

Behold, the Kingdom of God is within you.

The window dissolves. You see a frosted landscape beneath the midnight winter sky. The trees and bushes are bare of leaves. The air is crystal clear. The night is moonless and the stars shine like a great sea of light across the heavens. You begin to pick out the constellations in their turning. You see them revolving like a great luminous wheel around the pole star. Looking back at the landscape you see, standing at the crest of a hill, a mighty bull. Cold breath snorts from its nostrils as it paws the ground releasing a rolling torrent of gems and crystals which gather in a heap of resplendent treasure at the foot of the hill. You see starlight reflecting in the multitude of shining stones. Then, the bull turns ageless eyes towards you in the utter clarity of impartial wisdom. And you salute the mighty Kerubic creature of the North.

Over the entire scene, be aware of the presence of the Archangel Auriel, robed in dark indigo light with sparks of brilliant gold and silver flashing here and there. He holds a crystal paten, cunningly engraved with the secret patterns of the universe. From this paten rises, like a stream of shooting stars, a host of angelic and elemental beings. You feel yourself momentarily filled with an intuitive awareness of the deepest cosmic mysteries.

You close the golden book and see the glass solidify into a dark softly glowing mass of variegated green and brown light which shows the image of a bull, and beneath it the word LAW.

(pause for meditation)

The room fades from vision and you are aware of yourself once more at the center of the celestial sphere. The sphere contracts, bringing the stars together until they unite. And you find yourself enclosed in an aura sized orb of pure starlight. You are aware, also, of the axis running through the poles of the orb; of the golden flame within your heart; and of the chalice woven out of the solar light of the flame.

Now, become aware of the sun chalice filling with light, which when it reaches the rim of the chalice, spills over in a great lightning flash that shoots out rays to the four directions: before and behind you, to your right and to your left; that is, to the East and to the West, to the South and to the North. As you meditate upon this

great cosmic cross radiating from your heart, you in-
tone an appropriate ritual phrase (*suggestions*: "A turning cross of life unfolding;" "Blessed are those upon
the Cross;" "Be hallowed by a turning cross.").

VI

The Three Worlds

According to a very ancient and widespread tradition, the Risen Christ gave out his secret name (or names) to the Apostles. In esoteric practice, the name of Christ constitutes a "Key to the Kingdom of Heaven," a secret name of power giving access to the mysteries of the Three Worlds and the Planes of Being: "God has highly exalted him and bestowed upon him the name which is above every name, that at the name of Jesus every knee should bow, in heaven and on earth and under the earth" (*Philippians 2:9-11*). We have made passing reference, throughout our previous chapters, to the idea of the Three Worlds or regions of the cosmos. These are generally referred to as the celestial world, the underworld, and the terrestrial world. We shall here take a more detailed look at their structure and importance for esoteric work.

When speaking of the terrestrial world we are not referring merely to the plane of physical phenomena. For from an esoteric point of view—and this is the only one which concerns us here—the terrestrial world includes what might be called an "etheric" dimension: Expressions and currents of spiritual energies are sensed or envisioned within the landscape. Certain features or constructs occurring or placed within the terrestrial sphere give access to certain innerworld or spiritual energies. The same distinctive elements provide nodal points of entry and exit for souls and psychic and spiritual energies flowing between the worlds.

Although visionary ascent to the celestial world or descent to the underworld may take place from any power site or magical node, certain types of sites or features lend themselves through their intrinsic symbolism to certain types of inner plane work and activity. Generally speaking, mountains, trees, hills, standing stones, towers, spires, pillars, mounds, indeed all those features which rise up, require climbing, ascending, or which otherwise draw the soul upwards, link with the celestial world. Indeed in many cases the physical act of ascending is accompanied by a ritual or visionary rising on the planes. Likewise the features of descent include caves, grottos, springs, valleys, rivers, wells, tombs, crypts, catacombs, and so on. We also note that features like caves, groves, temples and other sacred enclosures typically contain symbolism which points to both upper and lower worlds. And we have touched upon the universal significance of the tree as a symbol of the structure of all Three Worlds.

An interesting pattern of sacred caves and holy mountains occurs in the initiatory formula of the Magical Life of Christ:

Cave of Nativity	*Mount of Transfiguration*
Cave of Descent	
and Ressurection	*Mount of Crucifixion*
Cave of Ascension†	*Mount of Ascension*

Several of these features clearly express the tenor of the mysteries they are connected with: the Caves of the Nativity, and of the Descent relate to the mysteries of the underworld; the Mounts of the Transfiguration and Ascension relate to the celestial mysteries. The mount of the Crucifixion functions more as a nodal point, a symbolic center by which the entire creation, visible and invisible, is anchored, enabled and permeated with the Logoic presence.

The cave of the Ascension serves to point up the close relationship between the Cosmic Axis and the Center. Central nodes are always found upon the Axis, just as the axial images always

---

†According to Eusebius, who speaks of the "three sacred places revered for three mystical caves," the Ascension took place from a cave in the Mount of Olives.[51]

The Virgin of the Tree. This image carved into the trunk of a tree shows the sovereignty of the Holy Virgin Mother over the Three Worlds, but with special links to the underworld forces of latent manifestation. Church of San Felipe de Neri, Albuquerque, New Mexico.

point to (or run through) the Center. Particular images merely serve to emphasize either the axial or nodal power in a given sacred site.

Taken together, the three sacred caves of Christian lore lead us deep into the mysteries of the Divine Feminine. Caves represent the dark womb of creation, the fecund center of pure potentiality whence all manifest form arises. Another facet of the archetype of the Divine Feminine is found in the traditions relating to the Holy Virgin Mother. In Magical Christianity, the Holy Mother appears in three main guises corresponding to the Three Worlds. There is the aspect of the terrestrial Mary, appearing in the roles of:

1) Mother of Jesus.

2) Leader of the Apostles after the Resurrection who brought to birth the Christian Mysteries.

3) The redeemed Eve, that is, as an incarnation of the spirit of Life,† "the sleeping virgin now awakened."

†The word "Eve" literally means "Life."

The Celestial Virgin seated upon the Star Throne. From a mosaic at San Apollinare Nuovo, Ravenna.

The Celestial Virgin surrounded by stars and angels. Window at Chartres.

The figure of Mary takes on even higher and deeper implications when contacted in her aspects of Star Maiden and Black Virgin. We give below a summary of the type of energies and polarities we are dealing with in these two figures:

Black Madonna	Celestial Virgin
Mater Dolorosa	Queen of Heaven
Crystals, metals	Stars, planets
Elemental beings	Angelic beings
Transmission of tradition through bloodlines	Spiritual transmission of tradition
Martyrs, Champions, and Hermits	Virgins, Saints, and Magi
The Taker	The Giver
The Unraveller	The Weaver
The way to the Earthly Paradise	The way to the New Jerusalem
Underworld	Celestial World

Obviously these correspondences offer a perspective rather different from the usual trivialized notions of "heaven and hell" doled out by the conventional Church. In Magical Christianity, the underworld descent complements the celestial ascent. In its pure form, the underworld journey corresponds with a "hard way" of initiation and may even result in instantaneous illumination. It is the way of the warrior or spiritual knight and requires in good measure the personal characteristics of strength, courage, initiative, action, skill, and self-sacrifice.

In the *Divine Comedy*, Dante has a vision of the Church Militant in the earthly paradise and the Church Triumphant in the highest visible sphere of the heavens. These two facets of the Inner Church, for reasons we shall shortly discover, correspond to the underworld and celestial world journeys respectively. Underlying Dante's great initiatory poem, then, is the traditional model of Three Worlds or cosmic regions. There are several ways of viewing this structure within the *Comedy*.

A Black Virgin of the
Pillar - France.

Black Virgin of Montserrat,
Spain. Replica from the
author's collection.

One way is to see the underworld as a purely demonic experience, the terrestrial experience as a purgatorial journey of suffering, and the celestial journey as an extension of the purgatorial, with ever refined levels of purity and spiritual vision leading in the end to a divine vision and then a return to the earthly sphere. A variant on this—one which fits the intrinsic structure of the poem better—would see the celestial mysteries in essentially the same manner: as a rising on the planes until, at the highest levels, the vision fails or is swept aside by the unfathomable reality of Divine Being. The *Purgatorio,* however, and to some extent the *Paradiso* also, would be envisioned as an initiatory scenario that occurs simultaneously with, or even alternative to, the *Inferno.* In other words on one level the ascent of Mount Purgatory is also a descent to the underworld, and simultaneously a rising through the celestial spheres. We see this reflected in the integral structure of Dante's Worlds. The mount of purgatory occupies the same "space" as the pit of hell. The journey past the guardian at the center of the earth is, in a way, simultaneously a passage into the earthly paradise.

In actual initiatory experience there is normally a certain crossing over or shifting between spheres of experience. Certain aspects of the experience will have to do with underworld factors, others with celestial contacts, and yet others with one's view of the terrestrial world. Because so much depends upon the development of the individual soul, there is no telling beforehand exactly what this mix of energies will be or, for that matter, how the soul will react to them. For any given individual the nature of this experience really depends upon factors like spiritual integrity, personal destiny, courage, and a willingness to change for the better and to surrender the personal ego to a higher cause. To the degree the candidate is stubborn or flexible, egotistical or humble so will he or she experience alternatively the sufferings of hell,† the cleansing of purgatory, the wholeness of paradise, or the illumination of heaven. This is why mystery training is often so long and hard. To expose an unprepared soul to the powerful forces evoked during ritual initiation could indeed wreak havoc with that individual's personal life.

†Remember, all of the souls in Dante's *Inferno* are there because they ultimately refuse to change for the better.

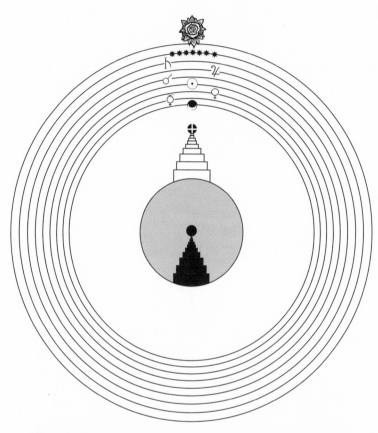

Dante's Cosmos as depicted in his initiatory poem, the *Divine Comedy.* The Mount of Purgatory with the earthly paradise on its peak is formed of the earth which was displaced by the fall of Lucifer who lies head down at the center of the pit of Hell. Just as the Holy Mount is the higher aspect of the nether regions, so is the pattern of the Celestial Spheres a higher octave of the Mount of Purgatory.

The idea that paradise or the "Edenic state" can be reached through a descent to the underworld is not exclusive to Dante by any means. One sees the same process in certain of the very early lives of the saints, such as those of Macarius and Onuphrius, who journeyed perilously through the desert to live in caves, or tombs which were said to be located at the shortest possible distance from paradise. Also interesting are the medi-

Christ in the underworld

eval legends and tales which grew up around a cave on an island in Lough Derg, Ireland. Labeled *St. Brendan's Purgatory* or more popularly *St. Patrick's Purgatory,* the cave was widely known in medieval times and attracted pilgrims from all over Europe. There was an abbey on the site and entry to the cave was gained, with permission of the abbot, through a special door located behind the high altar of the church. Tradition held that spending a night within this cave would absolve the pilgrim from the need to pass through purgatory after death. In other words it was a resolution of past (one is tempted to say *karmic),* "sins" or responsibilities, a living initiation here and now. It was common for the pilgrims to experience powerful visions during the ordeal. It is even said that some never returned from the cave having vanished into the otherworld. One of the more famous pilgrims (one who did return!) was Owain Miles or Owain the Knight whose tale is worth summarizing.

Owain was an English knight who had lived a life of dissipation and violence. In repentance he sought out the cave at Lough Derg that he might be purged of his sin and guilt. For fifteen days at the Abbey he engaged in preliminary devotions and alms-deeds. Then he attended Mass, was baptized, received the Sacrament, and followed the reliquary procession while the priests sang the litany. The door behind the altar was opened and he entered the darkness of the cave.

Sir Owain groped his way in the dark until he saw a glimmer of light. This grew brighter and brighter until he found himself in an inner land. Here there was a great hall and cloister peopled by men with shaven heads and white robes. They instructed Owain as to how to protect himself against evil spirits. Having received his instruction the Knight heard a great din and found himself in the midst of an onslaught of devilish beings. Using the teaching he had received for protection, however, he made his way further into the depths. At one point he was pushed into a pit of molten metal by negative spirits, but escaped when he called upon the name of the Savior. He crossed a river of boiling pitch by means of a narrow frail bridge, then came before a wall of glass, or crystal, in which was set a beautiful gate. Through this gate he came upon the Land of Paradise. This was so wondrous a place that the knight would have stayed if he could, but he was asked to return to the terrestrial world.

And so return he did, but by a shorter, more pleasant path than that by which he had come. Owain was found at the door the next morning, waiting to be let out that he might recount his adventure. He afterwards went on a pilgrimage to the Holy Land and ended his days a man of renowned spirituality.

The spiritual knight who would descend to the paradise, needs preparation. In the story of Owain this takes the form of a special Mass, which ends with the knight being "sung" into the underworld cave. There he meets inner helpers, Inner Plane Adepti, who convey special knowledge or power to the candidate without which he could not succeed or endure the ordeal. Yet this knowledge requires the ability to set aside the ego, to surrender oneself to the divine being for it is this which ultimately "saves." There is likely an intended alchemical symbolism or resonance in the knight's ordeal of molten metal. Like the Great Work of the alchemist, the regeneration of the soul can only be finally attained with divine aid. It is no more possible to pull oneself through the underworld by one's own power than it is to lift oneself into heaven by one's bootstraps. Owain attains the paradisal realm and emerges a transformed being. The way back is easy and pleasant because the Knight has succeeded in redeeming the unregenerate aspects of his soul.

All this ties in with traditional esoteric teaching regarding the Dweller on the Threshold. The Dweller on the Threshold is the guardian entity which blocks the initiate's passage through the portal of the Mysteries. Such figures exist on several levels, but the common teaching is that the Dweller reflects the unredeemed elements of one's own soul. Normally one must acknowledge, accept and learn to live with these elements, and by so accepting (far harder than it sounds), finds they are "redeemed." But this encounter rarely takes the form of frightening visions. Instead it is generally experienced through events, relationships, emotions, desires, etc., that arise in the course of daily life.

The underworld journey involves, then, a coming to terms with the "lower" levels of (one's) being, a resolution of the drag of patterns of the past—usually from beyond the present life— and of a reconnecting with the Edenic state of existence. In very practical terms, this means clarifying and generally reconfiguring one's relationship to creation and to one's fellow creatures. The obviously exemplary pattern for all this is Christ's Descent to the Underworld by means of which "death and hell" were conquered and the way opened to paradise. We have given an outline of the cosmic significance of this pattern in Chapter v.

The Magical Life of Christ, it will have been noticed, involves the expression of divine mysteries equally in all Three Worlds or cosmic regions. At the same time, however, the incarnational nature of Christianity emphasizes the living out or manifestation of these archetypal energies within the situations of daily life. In fact, the further one progresses along the path of the Christian Mysteries, the more important is the way in which one approaches daily life in general. As is exemplified in the pattern of the Christ life, the most profound mysteries are sometimes "worked out" *incognito* and in the midst of apparently insignificant circumstances.

Even so, there can be little doubt that the oft referred to secret teachings given the Apostles by Christ included tuition on the descent and ascent of the soul through the various worlds

The Ascension. Christ rising into the Empyrean. From a 10th century German Bible.

and planes. Not only was this in the form of a "Book of the Dead" giving instruction for the passage of the soul after death, but quite obviously included teaching relating to the practice of "rising on the planes." Paul, for instance, speaks of rising to the "third heaven." This teaching appears sporadically (it was, after all, secret) in texts like *The Ascension of Isaiah*, *The Apocalypse of Peter* (which is contemporary with *Revelations*), and *The Apocalypse of Paul*. Such texts are not always easy to read for their teachings about visionary ascent and descent through the worlds, are often mixed with hellish stories of demons and damnation. In Magical Christianity, one learns to look beyond such negative images seeing them for what they really are: largely deterrents or safeguards deliberately placed to discourage indiscriminate experience of the inner worlds by the uninitiated. These safeguards are more the result of a spirit of compassionate protection rather than of any desire to exclude dedicated individuals from contacting the inner powers of the cosmos.

As we have said, behind these apocryphal tales is a visionary technique of rising on the planes. This technique was partially assumed into Christianity through Jewish *Merkabah* Esotericism—a forerunner of the Qabalah.

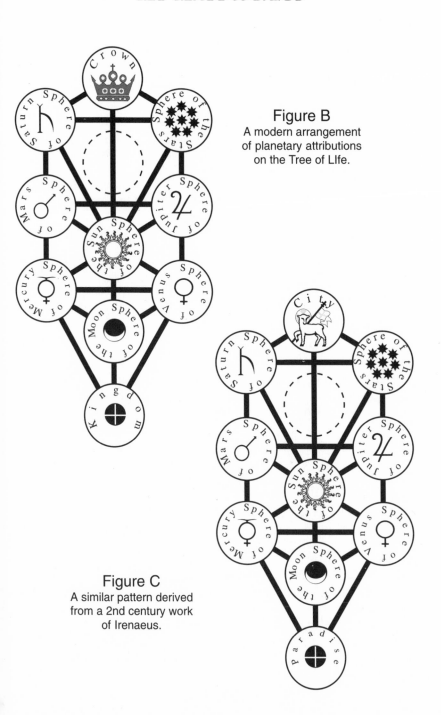

Figure B
A modern arrangement
of planetary attributions
on the Tree of Life.

Figure C
A similar pattern derived
from a 2nd century work
of Irenaeus.

All this brings us once more to the diagram of the Tree of Life. Most modern versions of the Tree show ten spheres indicating the relationships among various archetypal energies and states of being. On one level, these energies are expressed in terms of "planetary" spheres (Figure B).

A similar designation was apparently in use in the early stages of Christian Esotericism. Irenaeus writes of the three regions of "the heavens, the paradise and the city." [70,22] "The heavens" include the seven spheres of the visible planets and the *ogdoad* or realm of the stars. These eight, combined with "the paradise and the city" or New Jerusalem, yields a pattern of ten spheres (Figure C). An alternative or extended view would be to see the paradise as the underworld complement to the New Jerusalem with the spheres as the ways and means of traversing the worlds. In this view the terrestrial world becomes the point of manifestation for both the descending and ascending forces of creation. These powers are symbolized by the planets and stars of the celestial world on one hand, and on the other by the seven ancient metals and the crystals of the underworld (Figure D).

The actual technique of ascending through the spheres involves the assumption through ritual or vision of the spiritual qualities of each sphere successively. In Magical Christianity this is sometimes also expressed in terms of angelic beings or "states." Clement of Alexandria, for instance says that the gnostic soul successively traverses the heavenly spheres which correspond to the angelic orders. Taking on the form or state appropriate to the angelic nature of each sphere, the soul rises in contemplation until it achieves a lucid vision of the highest heaven. [71,22]

In modern magical visions and ritual, one finds a complex interplay of symbolic correspondences. Usually the energies associated with each of the Three Worlds are not worked with in their pure forms. Most Magical Christian practices employ symbols and energies drawn from all levels simultaneously. Normally, in other words, the Three Worlds are worked together with varying degrees of emphasis on each one according to the structure and purpose of the meditation, ritual or inner journey. Among other things this allows a more gradual and integrated passage through the relevant energies and experiences. We give below two exercises that may be performed on alternat-

the three worlds

Figure D

In Magical Christianity, the Tree of Life is a flexible diagram used to show relationships between archetypal energies. It provides a means of orientation, and a ground plan or itinerary for various forms of innerplane journeys, meditations, and rituals.

In the figure at left, the terrestrial world is indicated by the central sphere which shows a mountain and a cave—two features linking to the celestial and underworld powers respectively. The symbols of the planets, shown in the upper half of the diagram also appear in the lower half as the symbols of the seven sacred metals. These correlate as follows: Moon=Silver; Mercury=Quicksilver, Venus=Copper, Sun=Gold, Mars=Iron, Jupiter=Tin, Saturn=Lead. The spheres of the stars and the New Jerusalem in the Celestial Tree correspond to the spheres of the crystals and of Paradise in the Underworld Tree. The higher or deeper aspects of each of the two Trees are, in this case, reached through the intercession of the Holy Virgin Mother as either Star Maiden or Black Madonna.

Below: the Three Worlds, the Two Trees and the Egg of Creation.

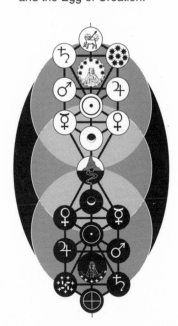

ing occasions. The first emphasizes the energies of the celestial world, the second emphasizes certain positive elements of the underworld experience. Both work through contact with the Holy Virgin Mother.

Exercise:
OUR LADY OF THE STARS

After the *Kenotic Opening,* proceed as usual, reciting the appropriate phrases as you build up the symbols of the previous exercises: *the Sphere of Creation, the Lance of Light, the Living Flame, and the Sun Chalice.*

As you say the ritual phrase for *the Secret Gospels,* the Chalice fills with light then spills over in a fourfold flash of light to the four directions.

You find yourself in the stone chapel, with each of its four walls dominated by a tall massive, arched window filled with stained glass. You see the four closed books resting on stone lecterns each facing one of the great windows.

You are standing facing the East and you notice near each corner of the wall a carved wooden door. The door near the right hand corner attracts your attention because it has a lighted lamp hanging before it. You approach the door which you see is carved with the patterns of the stars and the symbols of the planets. You take the lamp from its hook and with the other hand open the door. It swings inward and you see a winding stair leading up within the thick stone walls of the chapel. You ascend the stair and come out upon the roof of the chapel.

Breathing in the cool night air, you look around you and see to one side a stone shrine containing a magnificent statue of the Holy Virgin Mother. She is seated upon a throne of dark stone and has a veil and a cloak studded with stars. On her lap she holds an image of the Christ Child. In one hand the Child holds a globe with the celestial map engraved upon it. The other hand, raised in blessing, points toward the heavens.

You allow your gaze to move upward to the wondrous sea of stars in the sky above. There, standing in the heavens, you see a great figure of the Holy Virgin, Our Lady of the Stars. At her feet a dragon of rainbow light entwines itself about the polestar writhing and undulating in flashes of variegated color.

From the outstretched hands of the Star Mother come threads of light which flash out amongst the stars, linking them into patterns which you recognize as the various constellations. And now into one hand she receives the seven rays of the seven ancient planets: an Indigo ray of Saturn, a blue ray of Jupiter, a red ray of mars, a golden ray of the Sun, a green ray of Venus, an orange ray of Mercury, and a silver ray of the Moon.

From her other hand, the purified rays of light descend to you, filling you with an intuitive awareness of deep cosmic principles: of the relationship between the shape and significance of the landscape and the patterns and power of the stars, as well as the meaning of the planets and their occult influence and relationship to your body and soul.

Having been baptized in these celestial powers, you raise the lamp in salute to the Lady of the Stars, then kneel for a few moments in contemplation before the Shrine of the Virgin and Child. You rise and make you way down the spiral stair to the Chapel. You close the carved door and hang the lamp in its place.

The chapel fades from vision and you find yourself at the center of the star sphere. The sphere contracts, bringing the lights together until you are enclosed in an aura-sized globe of pure starlight. You become aware of the axis running through the poles of the sphere; of the golden flame within your heart; and of the chalice woven out of the light of the flame. The chalice fills with light, which when it reaches the rim, spills over in a great lightning flash to the four directions.

And now, become aware, just above your head, of a shining crown of seven stars. And as you meditate upon the meaning of this symbol, recite the relevant ceremonial phrase (*suggestions*: "A starry crown of seven rays;" "Blessed are those who touch the stars;" "Be hallowed by a starry crown.").

Exercise:
OUR LADY OF THE CRYSTALS

After *the Kenotic Opening,* proceed as usual, reciting the appropriate phrases as you build up the symbols of the previous exercises: *the Sphere of Creation, the Lance of Light, the Living Flame, and the Sun Chalice.*

As you say the ritual phrase for *the Secret Gospels,* the Chalice fills with light then spills over in a fourfold flash of light the four directions.

You are again in the stone chapel looking towards the eastern wall. This time, you notice that the lamp hangs over the door near the lefthand corner. Approaching the door, which is inset with gems and precious metals, you take the lamp from its peg. You open the door, and pass onto a stair which winds downward into the earth.

You come out into a dark cave or crypt beneath the chapel. To one side you see a shrine containing a statue of a Black Virgin and Child. Their golden robes are studded with gems and crystals. The image of the Child has in one hand a crystal sphere etched with geometric patterns, while the other hand points downward in blessing. You follow the direction with your vision and see at the foot of the shrine, safeguarded by a wrought iron grill in the form of a *vesica piscis*, a deep well or fissure in the earth. You lower your lamp and look into the well.

The light reflects from a myriad of shining crystals which flash like a sea of stars in the great cavern beneath you. Amidst the light of the crystals forms a figure of the Holy Virgin, Our Lady of the Crystals. Beneath her feet a rainbow dragon undulates in flashes of variegated light. The Virgin extends her arms, sending out threads of light into the earth itself, weaving the crystals together in the pattern of a great latticework of energy flowing through the very fabric of the land. You realize that the points where the threads of the lattice of light join together mark the locations of all sacred sites throughout the world.

And now, into one hand, the Mother draws the energy of the seven sacred metals: an indigo ray of Lead, a blue ray of Tin, a red ray of Iron, a golden ray of Gold, a green ray of Copper, an orange ray of Quicksilver, and a silver ray of Silver. Then from her other hand, a pure light shoots upward, filling you with deep cosmic awareness of the principles of creation and existence. These you realize are active and accessible within the land and within your body and soul.

Having been bathed in this fountain of energy, you move your lamp in salute to the Virgin and then kneel briefly in contemplation before the shrine of the Mother and Child. You rise and return up the spiral stair to the Chapel. As you close the door and hang the lamp in its place, the chapel fades from vision.

You are once again at the center of the cosmic sphere. The sphere contracts, bringing the stars together until you are encompassed by an aura-sized globe of starlight. You are aware of the axis running through the poles of the sphere; and of the golden flame within your heart. Out of the light of the flame appears the chalice.

This itself fills with light, which when it reaches the rim, spills over in a great lightning flash to the four directions.

Above your head you are aware of the shining crown of seven stars. And now you become aware, in complement to the crown, of a great crystal throbbing with power in the earth beneath your feet. As you meditate upon the meaning of the symbols, you recite the appropriate ritual phrase (*suggestions*: "A crystal stone of sure foundation;" "Blessed are those who find the stone;" "Be hallowed by a crystal stone.").

VII

the
planes of being

The concept of a three-tiered universe is found in nearly all spiritual traditions and has many forms and nuances. The pattern of the Three Worlds is one of these. It is one which fits, however, into the much larger pattern of the Planes of Being. This threefold pattern comprises the material or physical plane, the intermedial or magical plane, and the spiritual or archetypal plane. These three planes resonate with the threefold constitution of the human being. The material plane correlates with the physical body, the magical plane with the soul, and the archetypal plane with the spirit. We might further link the planes and the human constitution with three modes of perception. The material level corresponds to sensation, and discursive or analytical reason. The magical plane corresponds to the inner, psychic or prophetic senses, to symbolic thinking, and to what we might call the "imaginal" faculty. The archetypal level corresponds to higher modes of philosophical thought, to mystical apprehension and spiritual intuition. Let us look in more detail at each of the planes.

The material plane deals with sensory facts, with physical objects, with the use of reason to draw inference from sensory data. Viewed from the flatland of its own level, the physical plane embodies a perspective which determines reality solely in quantitative terms. This is the position of reductive materialist science or "scientism" as it is sometimes called. There is, from this point of view, an attempt to reduce reality to biological terms,

The Planes of Being here shown as
three successive spheres ruled over by
the Cosmic Christ. From a medieval
book cover.

The Planes of Being. The Monogram of Christ in the
form of a six-pointed cross traverses three spheres.
Dome in the baptistery at Albenga, Italy.

and a tendency therefore to view the world as mechanistic and meaningless, and to see human life as devoid of any higher or deeper significance or interpretation. The scientistic experience tends to awaken the characteristics of narrowness, materialism, greed, and a general disdain for one's fellows (who are, after all, merely objects, or randomly "evolved" organisms in a purposeless world). In other words, the material plane perspective spawns an essentially soulless existence without design or meaning.

Unfortunately this is fast becoming the common standard by which people judge reality in the modern West. Relatively few people nowadays admit the existence of the magical plane. And the spiritual plane is generally consigned a vague, distant significance-one considered hardly relevant for life in the "real world" except perhaps to be touted as a "source" for literal minded moralism or rigid behavioral precepts. No matter how strongly its existence is denied, however, the two thirds of creation corresponding to the magical and archetypal planes will not be ignored. Thus one sees in modern society the irruption of the "New Age" movements. Though these appear generally spurious or superficial to serious practitioners of traditional magical and spiritual ways, they nonetheless serve to reconnect popular consciousness to inner reality-albeit in a tenuous, incomplete, camouflaged, or even degenerate manner. But even a weak and dangerously frayed connection is better than none at all.

One of the reasons the spiritual plane seems so inaccessible to many people is their disavowment of the reality of the magical or intermedial plane. "The structure of reality is such that it is not possible to move from one end to the other unless one passes through the middle," wrote Thomas Aquinas.† The magical plane is the middle plane, the plane of mediation. It allows us simultaneously to reach both towards spiritual reality and the physical environment in meaningful ways. Those who learn to operate from this plane find that it transfigures the material reality, imbuing it with depth, meaning, and power. Certain features of the landscape, certain aspects of architecture, certain areas of the human physiology assume an occult significance

---

†Ordo rerum talis esse invenitur, ut ab uno extremo ad alterum non pervenientur nisi per media.

The Planes of Being conceived of as spheres within spheres. Beyond all planes, yet simultaneously encompassing, permeating and generating the whole of creation, is Deity which is variously depicted here as: Ultimate Being-that which epitomizes all being, Infinite Being-that which embraces all being, Non Being-that which is beyond all being.

and connectedness, becoming portals to unseen energies and realities. The magical plane ensouls the physical plane and by it the great web of nature is vivified. Through it the various kingdoms of nature- mineral, vegetative and animal-become active and significant. It is thus the plane of the totem animals, of herbal correspondences, of healing stones, and the like. It deals also with the inner senses, with mythic and symbolic thought and perception, with unseen forces and "spiritual" beings, with prophecy, vision, psychic abilities and magical powers. Prima-

The Planes of Being, the Two Trees, and the Three
Worlds. Only the highest and deepest levels of the
Tree touch upon the archetypal plane, here
symbolized by a circle of abstract figures.

rily a plane of symbols and energies, the magical realm is characterized, among other things, by a certain fluidity. It has its
own structure and principles, but these are not of such a nature
as to yield their secrets to mechanical or quantitative observation. It is, of course, the plane of the Three Worlds which were
the subject of Chapter vi: the terrestrial world or transfigured
physical plane† (which has both a visible and invisible aspect),
the celestial world which deals with visionary symbolism of an
ascensional nature, and the underworld which deals with visions of a descensional nature

Those who actively engage the magical plane inevitably find
themselves in contact with "inner" beings of various kinds. There
are generally three types of beings one might encounter on this
plane. Those that are beneficial to the human soul; those that

†Each plane "contains" and transforms the planes below it.

are neutral to human well-being; and those that are inimical to humanity. Clearly the forces of the magical plane should not to be invoked indiscriminately, that is, without proper orientation, guidance and protection.† For obvious reasons the Mystery Traditions of the world tend to concern themselves primarily with those inner plane contacts that have the well-being of humanity at heart or which can benefit from positive contact with human consciousness: Masters, saints, heroes, goddesses and gods, figures from myth and legend, and historical figures whose lives carried archetypal patterns, boddhisatvas, devas, power animals, faeries, elementals, angels, and the list goes on. Before considering some of the beings which play a role in esoteric Christian tradition, it will be useful to look at the subject of beneficent inner plane contacts from a general perspective. One way to do this is by considering the various beings in terms of their spiritual function or role. We may say, then, that there are those beings who operate primarily as *guides*, those that operate mainly as *guardians*, and those who operate as *intercessors*.‡

Inner guides are characterized by their concern with communication between the planes. They invariably offer some form of useful message or teaching. They are the inner teachers, counselors and way showers. The actual process of communication may take various forms. It may involve mediumship where the physical body is temporarily given over to the control of an inner guide. Or it may work through the perceptions of the inner senses. One might for instance "hear" the teaching or see an inner guide in vision. Or one might simply sense the presence of a guide, and then pay particular attention to thoughts, images and ideas which happen arise in the mind. These may then be translated into verbal or visual form. Alternatively, a guide could appear in the inner vision to take one upon a magical journey. In this case the message might be encoded in the symbolism of the images and experience itself. Sometimes, communication occurs through meaningful coincidence, or "signs following." This involves paying attention to the inherent symbolism of

---

†This is one facet of the role and value of the mystery schools, which provide time-tested methodology, philosophy and ethics for dealing with the energies and entities of the inner planes.

‡For a more detailed look at the three orders of contact see my book *Contacting Spiritual Beings*.

certain happenings in daily life, intuitively deciphering from them relevant teaching and guidance.

Guardians are beings who preserve and protect human beings, sacred sites, secret teachings and Holy Mysteries. There are many levels or aspects to the role of Guardianship. There are, on one hand those beings whose function it is to protect people either individually, that is on a one to one basis, or collectively on the basis of an individual's association with a sacred site, temple, lodge or magical order.

On the other hand, inner guardian beings are also involved in protecting sacred sites and ritual workings from disturbance by the curious or unworthy. In mystery rituals, the guardian being (or beings) is closely associated with the office of Doorkeeper. The Doorkeeper is a special commission which hinges on the development of a particular relationship between the soul of the individual who holds the office and the guardian spirit of the Lodge.

Sacred sites have always had their *genii locorum*, their guardian spirits. Although modern Man's estrangement from the magical plane has left the landscape relatively impoverished in terms of acknowledged sacred sites, there are some sites where guardian beings are still active and many others where they are merely dormant. For this reason, discretion is required when visiting some of the sites, even where these may seem to have degenerated into little more than benign tourist attractions.

The guardians' power to deter has much to do with what used to be called "enchantment." Enchantment is in some ways similar to the modern notion of "psychological projection" in that it involves beholding in others a reflection of the unacknowledged aspects of our own souls. So far as the warding energies sometimes contacted at sacred sites are concerned, this usually means the unredeemed or negative elements of oneself. This can be quite the disturbing experience it is meant to be, for it usually affects the relationships with those whom one holds dear or who are otherwise closely connected to the activities of one's daily life. Family, friends, career or employment relationships are the usual pegs upon which is hung the mirror of enchantment.

As we noted in Chapter vi, the same process is behind what is known in the Mystery teachings as facing the Dweller on the

Threshold-a fearsome entity who traditionally stands at the portal of initiation, guarding the passage from the Lesser to the Greater Mysteries. Although active on several levels beyond that of personal psychology, the Dweller is commonly considered to embody the negative aggregate of one's soul. Facing or passing the Guardian on the Threshold requires that we accept, sublimate or redeem the unbalanced aspects of ourselves. This can be relatively easy or hard depending on the courage, integrity, and willingness to change of the aspirant.

It will be noted from all this that guardians in general are very much concerned with maintaining the distinction between Sacred and profane. This distinction is not one that occurs primarily in objects or places themselves, but in the attitudes and spiritual integrity of those who would approach sacred matters: "Hekas, hekas, estoi babeloi!" resounds the opening of the ancient mysteries "Begone, profane ones!"

Intercessors are inner beings who are concerned with aiding in the mediation of unseen forces and inner energies between the Three Worlds and the Planes of Being. They inevitably work in concert with incarnate humans to enable the relay of archetypal and ultimately beneficent forces and patterns from the inner planes into the sphere of human consciousness and activity. They are the great beings associated with healing, both of individuals and of groups, even up to the level of planetary healing.

Intercessors play an important role in theurgical ritual. Technically speaking, ritual involves the setting up of inner conduits through which spiritual power is enabled to flow from one plane of reality of another. This is why ritual, properly understood, always builds upon a general symbolic pattern representing simultaneously the spiritual structure of the cosmos and the constitution of the human being. The pattern of correspondences thus laid down enables mediation to take place. Mediation occurs through the principle of resonance or attunement. A particular sequence of symbols, built up in the inner vision,† enables consciousness to "vibrate" at a certain level, thus becoming a potential channel for the energies of that level.

---

†And, if in a ritual context, simultaneously arranged or presented on the external plane.

Christ as Guide. From a stained glass window.

Like the guardians, the intercessors are sometimes associated with sacred sites. But whereas the guardians are there to keep unwanted influences out and desired ones safe, the intercessors are concerned with enabling a flow of energy to take place within the protected confines of sacred space.

Let us recall that our division of beings into guides, guardians, and intercessors is based upon relationships between inner beings and incarnate humans. Specific entities may therefore function variously, or even simultaneously in all three "orders." We shall see examples of this shortly.

In ancient and Magical Christianity, the orders of beings who perform the functions of guides, guardians, and intercessors are encountered in various forms including the angelic hierarchies, the Virgin Mary, the saints and martyrs, animal beings, and ultimately the Christ. It is Christ in whom all being is subsumed and who therefore generates and epitomizes the roles of Guide, Guardian and Intercessor. Similarly, the Virgin Mary bears the titles of Intercessor, Protector, and Guide. To a lesser degree the Archangels also embody the functions of all three orders.

The Holy Virgin Mother as guardian protector of souls.
From a 13th century bas-relief.

Michael, for instance, is guide as Psychopomp, guardian as Angel before the Gate of Paradise, and intercessor as the presence presiding over the powers of a vast network of holy places. It is perhaps in reference to an archangel or to a "guardian angel" that the fourth century writer, Synesius of Cyrene, directs the following hymn:

> And give me a companion, O King, a partner, a sacred messenger of sacred power, a messenger of prayer illumined by the divine light, a friend, a dispenser of noble gifts, a guard of my soul, a guard of my life, a guard over prayers, a guard over deeds."[8]

It was common in ancient Christianity for saints to appear as inner guides to select individuals.† Gregory Thaumaturgus, for

---

†This is the origin of the adoption of Christian names. The taking on of the name of a saint was part of a process of bringing the soul under the protection and guidance of that saint.

instance, mentions being guided and nurtured by an inner presence. The Christian poet, bishop and imperial arbitrator, Paulinus of Nola, frequently received guidance from the spirit of Saint Felix.[8] Accounts of intercession of the martyred saints are also numerous. In the case of the martyrs, who carried on the ancient traditions of heroes and sacred kings, their power of intercession was closely linked to the sanctuaries or martyria which housed their remains. The heroic saints were believed to be somehow merged with their sacred sites. Their holy presence, being both immediate and transcendent, enabled them to function as mediatory beings between divine reality and terrestrial human life. This powerful intercessory experience came eventually to be applied to the saints in general, not just the martyrs. And so it became important that every altar be founded upon the relics of a saint.

As the traditions of the Communion of Saints spread through Christendom, certain magical practices developed alongside them. Until the end of the Middle Ages, for instance, people commonly engaged in *incubation*, which involved sleeping inside a sanctuary or church in order to receive healing and guidance given in a dream vision of the patron saint.[8]

In addition to the saints and martyrs, angelic beings play an important part in Magical Christian practice. As we have noted elsewhere, they are particularly important for the role they play in the techniques of "rising on the planes." The traditions of angelic hierarchies were first crystallized in written form by Dionysios the Areopagate. For Dionysios there are nine angelic orders divided into three triads of three orders each. Interestingly, these triads correspond to the three Planes of Being. The lower triad of Principalities, Archangels and Angels corresponds to the (transfigured) physical plane; the middle triad of Dominions, Powers and Authorities corresponds to the magical plane; The upper triad of Seraphim, Cherubim and Thrones corresponds with the archetypal plane. For Dionysios each of the triads also expresses a corresponding spiritual process. The Principalities, Archangels and Angels rule over the process of purification. The Dominions, Powers and Authorities are over the process of illumination. The Seraphim, Cherubim and Thrones rule over the process of perfection. These in turn he links to a set of three grades or degrees of initiation in the Christian Mysteries. The degree of Deacon, is concerned with purification, that of Priest with illumination, and that of Bishop with perfection.†[25]

One has in all this the outline of a tradition of spiritual development that hinges on relationships between angelic beings and human consciousness. The intermediary assistance of angelic beings and of symbolic visions is necessary for our spiritual growth, says Dionysios, because "we lack the ability to be directly raised up to conceptual contemplations." [25] This brings us to the archetypal plane.

The archetypal plane has to do with essences, universals, and holisms, with ideals, virtues, and spiritual principles. It is the plane of what is generally called the "Divine Names." The Divine Names or attributes, then, are universal principles, or archetypes. Following a Qabalistic formula, one pattern of archetypal principles might be Perfection, Wisdom, Understanding, Love, Justice, Beauty, Power, Glory, Strength and Unity. None of these can be apprehended by human mentation or imagination, except "as in a glass, darkly." Only through contemplation or spiritual intuition can the universals be grasped in any real fashion. And even then it is quite impossible to express the experience, except imperfectly through spiritual conduct or symbolic imagery. Even the so called "Negative Theology," which claims to reject all images as inadequate cannot escape expressing itself through images—though they be images of darkness, emptiness, a dark cloud, etc.—all of which symbolize an experience or reality which cannot otherwise be expressed. Thus again we see the mediatory importance of the magical plane, this time as a means of access to the plane of archetypal ideas or essences.

Each plane can be said to encompass or transfigure the plane or planes below it. We saw how the physical plane is encountered in a more meaningful way when viewed from the magical level of experience. So too are the physical and magical planes transformed when vision has been washed in the pool of archetypal experience. The physical plane not only carries thenceforth, a magical significance, but also a spiritual dimension.

There are certain types of holy places, sacred images, or spiritual beings whose importance derives from their common participation in an archetype (that is in their universal essence on

†It might be useful to recall that the word "perfection" means simply "to be made whole."

the archetypal plane). All gods for instance, tend toward the One God, all goddesses toward the Great Goddess, all nodes or centers toward the cosmic Center, all axial images towards the universal Axis, and so on. It is a realization of this resonant property of creation that prompts the fifteenth century cardinal and mystical philosopher, Nicholas of Cusa, to remark of the ancient pagans, "they adored the Divinity in all the gods."[30] And Gregory of Palamas speaks of the transformed vision of those who have been "deified" or "divinized": "Miraculously, they see with a sense that exceeds the senses, and with a mind that exceeds mind, for the power of the spirit penetrates their human faculties, and allows them to see things which are beyond us." [43]

Moreover, the transformation of perception experienced in each of the Planes of Being involves a corresponding transfiguration in the appropriate layers of the human constitution. On the magical plane the hidden powers of the soul are reflected in the occult anatomy of man. On the archetypal plane spiritual energies are reflected in the mystical physiology of the human being. Quoting Palamas again: "[I]n spiritual man, the grace of the Spirit, transmitted to the body through the soul, grants to the body also the experience of things divine..."[43] All this ties in with the esoteric doctrine of "centers" which teaches the significance of certain areas of the physical body as focal points for occult and spiritual energies. The activation and unfoldment of the magical powers of the soul and the granting of the Gifts of the Spirit, lies behind the secret teaching on the "Resurrection Body." We are speaking of the transfiguration, deification, or redemption of the human being on all levels-and this not as an eschatological hope, as in the exoteric doctrines, but as an immediate experience available to the initiate *hic et nunc.*

Successive experience of each of the Planes of Being brings the initiate closer to Ultimate Being. This is because each plane is qualitatively higher than the one below it. In other words it more closely approaches or embodies completion, wholeness, and therefore holiness. The "lower" planes are never left behind, but they are transfigured. The Fall of Man constitutes estrangement from the primordial wholeness of the Edenic state. The Redemption of Man means restoration to a life lived from the spiritual plane. Then shall "the very God of peace sanctify you wholly...spirit, soul and body."(*1Thessalonians 5:23*)

Exercise:

Note: The exercise given below comprises a ritual synthesis of the concourse of energies evoked through the practical work of the previous chapters. It works something like a magical rosary or chaplet. Indeed, it might be useful to construct or purchase a chaplet of seven (or a multiple of seven) beads as an enhancement to the exercise. Observe that the exercise is built upon the suggested ritual phrases which were given at the end of each of the preceeding chapters. The litany is composed of several sections: opening and closing invocations bracket an evocation of the seven symbols, a set of beatitudes, and a hallowing sequence. Operational notes on the various sections follow the text of the litany.

A LITANY OF LIGHT

{light central candle}
Let there be Light.
{raise right hand above head then touch forehead}
In the Name of the High Father,
{touch navel}
And of the Deep Mother,
{left shoulder, then right shoulder}
And of the Son of Light,
{bringing palms together before heart}
One Light, One Life, One Eternal Spirit.
Amen

May Being be blessed and sanctified
by this chaplet of seven sacred symbols:

A shining sphere of cosmic love,
Amen
A piercing ray of deepest peace,
Amen
A holy fount of living fire,
Amen
A chalice in the sacred heart,
Amen
A turning cross of life unfolding,
Amen
A starry crown of seven rays,
Amen
A crystal stone of sure foundation,
Amen

Upon the Way of Light.

Blessed are those who are centered in Love,
   For theirs is the Kingdom of Light. {*light candle 1*}
Blessed are those transfixed by Peace,
   For theirs is the Kingdom of Light. {*light candle 2*}
Blessed are those who raise up the Fire,
   For theirs is the Kingdom of Light. {*light candle 3*}
Blessed are those who seek the Grail,
   For theirs is the Kingdom of Light. {*light candle 4*}
Blessed are those upon the Cross,
   For theirs is the Kingdom of Light. {*light candle 5*}
Blessed are those who touch the Stars,
   For theirs is the Kingdom of Light. {*light candle 6*}
Blessed are those who find the Stone,
   For theirs is the Kingdom of Light. {*light candle 7*}

Be hallowed by a sacred sphere,
Be hallowed by a piercing ray,
Be hallowed by a living fire,
Be hallowed by a holy grail,
Be hallowed by a turning cross,
Be hallowed by a starry crown,
Be hallowed by a crystal stone,

Upon the Path of Peace.

{raise right hand above head then touch forehead}
In the Name of the High Father,
{touch navel}
And of the Deep Mother,
{left shoulder, then right shoulder}
And of the Son of Light,
{bringing palms together before heart}
One Light, One Life, One Eternal Spirit.
Amen

NOTES ON THE EXERCISE

Opening and Closing Invocation:

This accompanies the visualization of a cross of light with a rosy flame at its center. The invocation of the High Father and Deep Mother serves to direct the spiritual will towards the ultimate resolution of opposites. This is done by presenting the spiritual paradox that height is equivalent to depth, and is ritually signified by the marking and visualization of a vertical axis of infinite length .

The term "Son of Light" is an ancient title of Christ appearing, among other places, in certain Syriac traditions of the Magi and the Birth of Christ. Within these traditions the light is of the archetypal plane and its manifestation or theophany is at the center of the story of the Star of Bethlehem. The breaking through of the archetypal light to the physical plane is signified by the ritual drawing and vision of a horizontal ray of light passing though one's heart. The invocation of the Spirit and the envisioning of a rosy flame in the heart signify the unification or joining of the vertical and horizontal "polarities" of the cross of light.

Evocation of the Seven Symbols:

This is an initial building up of the symbols of the previous chapters. The word "Amen," meaning simply "let it be" or "let it be so," should be slowly intoned, as it incorporates certain ancient sonic principles of mediation and manifestation.

The Beatitudes:

These are based upon the ritual rhythms inherent in the Beatitudes of the Sermon on the Mount. Again, the seven symbols are evoked. As the rubrics of the litany indicate, a candle may be lit for each of the Beatitudes. One might therefore arrange upon one's work space or altar a central white candle within a circle of seven candles of the colors of the spectrum. These could then be lighted in sequence.

The Hallowing:

The Hallowing or "making holy" is the third level of a three stage consecration of consciousness inherent in the litany. It is a simple and powerful expression of the spiritual will.

appendix

the
kenotic† opening

You are sitting comfortably, back straight, feet flat on the floor, your palms resting upon your thighs.

Begin with controlled, regular breathing (four counts per in-breath and four counts per out-breath). Be aware of the rhythmic attunement of your entire being to your breath, and recall that the breath symbolizes the movement of the Spirit.

Now consciously allow deep peace and stillness to penetrate the levels of your being one at a time. Still your physical body first: your tensions dissipate, your muscles relax, your heartbeat slows, and all the internal processes of your body function in quiescent harmony.

Now still your desires and emotions, allowing them to become harmonized, to be absorbed into the great flow of Being. Let your thoughts too become still. Concentrate only upon your breathing. Empty yourself of all else.

There is only the breathing, the rhythm of the Deep Peace.

†From the Greek *kenos*, "empty," with reference to the tradition that Christ "emptied himself" in order to incarnate (cf Phillipians 2:7). Thus the exercise above should be undertaken in an attitude of contemplation. Ultimately one empties oneself of all earthly distraction, that one may be filled with the Divine Presence.

BíblíographY

Author's note: *Although this is not an academic work, the nature of our subject has required the consultation of more than one obscure academic tome, and in some cases even the translation (or retranslation) of relevant traditions from original sources. Much of the following reference material is therefore unlikely to be of interest to the general reader.*

The more readily available or accessible texts are marked with an asterisk (*) Of these, titles marked with a double asterisk (**) are of special importance for our subject.

[1]*The Ante-Nicene Fathers,* 10 vols. Alexander Roberts and James Donaldson, eds. Edinburgh, 1868. vol. 8 *

[2]*Apocrypha and Pseudepigraphia of the Old Testament in English.* ed. R.H. Charles. Oxford: Clarendon, 1913.

[3]*The Apocryphal New Testament.* Montague James. Oxford: Clarendeon, 1924. *

[4]Baez Macias, Eduardo. *El Arcangel San Miguel.* Mexico : Universidad Nacional Autonoma de Mexico, 1979.

[5]Baring-Gould, S. (Sabine), 1834-1924.*Curious Myths of the Middle Ages.* London: Rivingtons, 1868. **

[6]Barnes, Johnathan. *Early Greek Philospohy.* New York: Penguin, 1987.

[7]*The Bhagavad-Gita.* trans. Georg Feuerstein. New Delhi: Arnold-Heinemann, 1981.

[8]Brown, Peter. *The Cult of the Saints.* Chicago: Universtity of Chicago Press, 1981.

[9]Burckhardt, Titus. *Art of Islam: language and meaning.* London: World of Islam Festival Pub. Co., 1976.

[10]Butler, Alban, 1711-1773. *Butler's Lives of the Saints.* Herbert Thurston and Donald Attwater, eds. New York : Kennedy, 1956.*

[11]Campbell, Joseph, ed.. *The Mysteries.* New York: Bollingen, 1955. *

[2]Charbonneau Lassay, Louis. *The Bestiary of Christ*. New York: Arkana, 1992. **

[13]Climacus, St. John. *The Ladder of Divine Ascent*. trans. Archimandrite Lazarus Moore. London: Faber And Faber, 1959.

[14]*The Cloud of Unkowing*, James Walsh, ed.. New York: Paulist Press, 1981 **

[15]Cohn, Robert L. *The Shape of Sacred Space*. Chico, California: Scholars Press, 1981.

[16]Corbin, Henry. *The Man of Light in Iranian Sufism*. trans. Nancy Pearson. London: Shamballa, 1978.

[17]Couasnon, Charles. *The Church of the Holy Sepulchre in Jerusalem*. London: Oxford University Press, 1974.

[18]Crétien de Troyes (12th cent.). *Perceval: the Story of the Grail*. trans. Nigel Bryant. Cambridge: D.S. Brewer, 1982.

[19]d'Alverny, M.T. *Alain de Lille: Textes Inedits*. Paris: J. Urin, 1965.

[20]Danielou, Jean. *Primitive Christian Symbols*. Baltimore, Helicon Press,1964.

[21]—*The Bible and the Liturgy*. Notre Dame, Indiana: University of Notre Dame, 1956.

[22]—"Traditions Secretes des Apotres." *Eranos-Jahrbuch* Vol 32 (1962): 199-215.

[23]Dante Alighieri (14th cent.). *The Divine Comedy*. trans. Dorothy L. Sayers. Baltimore: Penguin, 1949. **

[24]Davies, J.G.. *The Architectural Setting of Baptism*. London: Barrie and Rockliff, 1962.

[25]Dionysius,The Areopagite. *The Complete Works*. New York: Paulist Press, 1987. **

[26]Duchesne-Guillemin, Jacques. *Symbols and Values in Zoroastrianism*. New York: Harper and Row, 1966.

[27]Duncan, Anthony. *The Lord of the Dance*. UK: Helios, 1972 **

[28]Edsman, Carl-Martin. "Fire." *The Encyclopedia of Religion*. ed. Mircea Eliade. 15 Vols. New York: Macmillan, 1987.*

[29]—*Le Bapteme de Feu*. Uppsala: Almquist & Wiksells, 1940.

[30]Eliade, Mircea. *History of Religious Ideas*. Chicago : University of Chicago Press, 1978. *

[31]—*The Forge and the Crucible*. New York: Harper & Row, 1971.

[32]—*Images and Symbols*. New York: Sheed & Ward, 1961.

[33]—*Patterns in Comparative Religion*. New York: Meridian, 1958 *

[34]—*Rites and Symbols of Initiation*. New York: Harper & Row,1965.

[35]—*he Sacred and the Profane*. New York: Harcourt, Brace & World, 1959.

[36]—*Shamanism*. New York: Bollingen, 1964

[37]—*The Two and the One*. New York: Sheed and Ward, 1965

[38]Ephraem Syrus, Saint, 303-373. *The Book of the Cave of Treasures*. trans. E. A. Wallis Budge London : Religious Tract Society, 1927.

[39]Every, George. *Christian Mythology*. Feltham: Hamlyn, 1970*

[40]Fideler, David. *Jesus Christ, Sun of God*. Wheaton: Quest, 1993. *

[41]Gaer, Joseph. *The Lore of the New Testament*. Boston: Little, Brown, 1952. **

[42]Grattan, John Henry Grafton and Charles Joseph Singer. *Anglo-Saxon Magic and Medicine*. London: Oxford University Press, 1952.

[43]Gregory Palamas, Saint. *The Triads*. trans. John Meyendorff. New York: Paulist Press, 1983. **

[44]Guénon, René. *Aperçus sur L'Ésoterisme Chrétien*. Paris: Éditions Traditionelles, 1983.

[45]*The Symbolism of the Cross*. London: Luzac, 1958. *

[46]Haavio, Marti. 'Vainamainen.' *Folklore Fellows Communication No. 144*. (1952).

[47]Hackwood, Frederick William. *Christ Lore*. Detroit: Gale Research Co., 1969.

[48]Hellbom, Anna-Britta. "The Creation Egg." *Ethnos*. No. 1 (1963).

[49]Hilton, Walter, d. 1396. *The Ladder of Perfection*. Harmondsworth: Penguin, 1957. *

[50]Hole, Christina. *Saints in Folklore*. London: Bell, 1966. *

[51]Hunt, E.D.. *Holy Land Pilgrimage in the Later Roman Empire AD 312-460*. Oxford: Clarendon Press, 1982.

[52]Ireneaus. *Epideixis, I*, 34. in J. A. Robinson (tr.) "The Demonstration of the Apostolic Preaching," London: 1920

[53]Isho, Anan. *The Paradise or Garden of the Holy Fathers.* trans. Sir E. A. Wallis Budge. New York: Duffield & company, 1909.

[54]Jacobus de Voragine. *The Golden Legend.* trans. Granger Ryan, Helmut Ripperger. New York: Longmans, Green and Co., 1941. *

[55]Johnson, Luke Timothy. *The Writings of the New Testament.* Philedelphia: Fortress Press, 1986.

[56]Julian of Norwich (15th cent.). *Showings.* New York: Paulist Press, 1978. *

[57]Jung, Emma & Von Franz, Marie-Louise. *The Grail Legend.* trans. Andrea Dykes. London: Conventure, 1970.

[58]Kahane, Henry & Renée. *The Krater and the Grail.* Urbana: University of Illinois Press, 1965.

[59]Knight, Gareth. *A Practical Guide to Qabalistic Symbolism.* Glos., UK: Helios, 1965 (reprinted by Samuel Weiser, NY.). *

[60]—*Experience of the Inner Worlds.* Glos., England: Helios, 1975 (reprinted by Samuel Weiser, NY, 1995.)**

[61]—*The Rose Cross and the Goddess.* Northhampshire, England: Aquarian, 1985. (new revised edition published by Destiny Books under the title *Evoking the Goddess*). **

[62]Lang, David Marshall. *Lives and Legends of the Georgian Saints.* New York: St. Vladimir's : 1956.

[63]Leone, Licia. *Simbolos místicos.* Buenos Aires: A. Pena Lillo, 1982.

[64]Lethaby, W.R.. *Architecture, Mysticism and Myth.* London: The Architectural Press, 1891.

[65]—*Architecture, Nature and Magic* London: Duckworth, 1956.

[66]MacCulloch, J. A.. *The Harrowing of Hell.* London: Clark, 1930.

[67]Martens, Mina. S*aint Michel et sa symbolique.* Brussels: Editions d'Art, Lucien De Meyer, 1979.

[68]Maximus the Confessor (7th cent.). *Selected Writings.* trans. George Berthold. New York: Paulist Press, 1985. *

[69]Mead, G.R.S.. *Quests, Old and New.* London: ????

[70]Migne, J.P. *Patrologia cursus completus Graeca.* Paris: Garnier Fratres, 1857. vol. 7

[71]—*Patrologia cursus completus Graeca.* Paris: Garnier Fratres, 1857. vol. 8

[72]—*Patrologia cursus completus Graeca.* Paris: Garnier Fratres, 1857. vol. 11

[73]—*Patrologia cursus completus Graeca.* Paris: Garnier Fratres, 1857. vol. 18

[74]—*Patrologia cursus completus Graeca.* Paris: Garnier Fratres, 1857. vol. 92

[75]—*Patrologia cursus completus Graeca.* Paris: Garnier Fratres, 1857. vol. 94

[76]—*Patrologia cursus completus Graeca.* Paris: Garnier Fratres, 1857. vol. 132

[77]—*Patrologia cursus completus Latina.* Paris: Garnier Fratres, 1844. vol. 4

[78]—*Patrologia cursus completus Latina.* Paris: Garnier Fratres, 1844. vol. 172

[79]—*Patrologia cursus completus Latina.* Paris: Garnier Fratres, 1844. vol. 173

[80]—*Patrologia cursus completus Latina.* Paris: Garnier Fratres, 1844. vol. 197

[81]Morgenstern, Julian. *The Fire Upon the Altar.* Chicago: Quadrangle Books, 1963.

[82]*Mythology of All Races.* New York: Cooper, 1964. Vol. 10

[83]*Myths and Symbols; studies in honor of Mircea Eliade.* Joseph Mitsuo Kitagawa, Charles H. Long, eds. Chicago: University of Chicago Press, 1969.

[84]Newall, Venetia. "Easter Eggs" *Folklore*, Vol 79 (winter, 1968) .

[85]Nicholas of Cusa (16th cent.). *de Ludo Globi.* "Nikolaus von Kues Werke, band III." Paul Wilpart, ed. Berlin: de Gruyer , 1967 : 575-625.

[86]O'Donnell, Timothy. *Heart of the Redeemer.* Manassas, Virginia: Trinity, 1989.

[87]Ohrt, F. "The Spark in the Water." *FF Communications* No. 65. 1926.

[88]Ortiz, Alfonso. *The Tewa World.* Chicago: University of Chicago Press, 1969.

[89]Parrot, André. *Golgotha and the Church of the Holy Sepulchre.* London: SCM Press, 1957.

[90]Pauphilet, A. (ed.). *La Quest du Saint Graal*. Paris, 1923.

[91]Pennick, Nigel. *The Ancient Science of Geomancy*. London: Thames and Hudson, 1979.   *

[92]Pettipierre, Francois. "The Symbolic Landscape of the Muiscas." *Studies in Comparative Religion* winter (1979) : 36-51.

[93]Polo, Marco. *The Description of the World*. trans. Moule and Rellot. London: Routledge and Sons, 1938.

[94]Rolle, Richard. *The Fire of Love*. trans. Clifton Wolters. New York: Penguin, 1972   *

[95]*The Secret Teachings of Jesus*. trans. Meyer, Marvin. New: York, Random House, 1984   *

[96]Sellner, Edward C.. *Wisdom of the Celtic Saints*. Notre Dame: Ave Maria, 1993. *

[97]Simson, Otto Georg von. *The Gothic Cathedral*. New York: Pantheon Books, 1956. *

[98]Smith, E. Baldwin. *The Dome*. Princeton: Princeton University Press, 1956.

[99]Smith, Johnathan Z.. "Earth And Gods." *The Journal of Religion* Vol 49, Number 2, (1969) :103-128.

[100]Stevenson, James. *The Catacombs: Life and Death in Early Christianity.* London: Thames and Hudson, 1978.

[101]Stewart, R.J. *The Elements of Creation Myth*. Shaftsbury, Dorset: Element, 1989. *

[102]—*The UnderWorld Initiation*. UK: Aquarian Press, 1985.*

[103]Stierli, Joseph ed. *Heart of the Savior*. New York: Herder, 1958.

[104]Teresa, of Avila, Saint, 1515-1582. *The Collected Works of St. Teresa of Avila*. Washington : Institute of Carmelite Studies, 1976. 25

[105]Thompson, Stith. *Tales of the North American Indians*. Bloomington: Indiana University Press, 1966.

[106]Vilnay, Zev. *Legends of Jerusalem*. Philedelphia: Jewish Publication Society of America, 1973.

[107]Walsh, David. *The Mysticism of Innerworldly Fufillment*. Gainesville: University of Florida, 1983.

[108]Watts, Alan. *Myth and Ritual in Christianity*. Boston: Beacon Press, 1968. *

[109]Wensinck, Arnet Jan. "The Ideas of the Western Semites Concerning the Navel of the Earth." *Verhandelingen der Koninklijke Akademie van Westenschappen*, 2nd series, XVII, no. 1, 1917.

[110]Whone, Herbert. *Church, Monastery, Cathedral*. Shaftsbury, Dorset: Element, 1990. **

[111]Wright, John Kirtland. *The Geographical Lore of the Time of the Crusades*. New York: American Geographical Society, 1925.

[112]Migne, J.P. *Patrologia cursus completus Graeca*. Paris: Garnier Fratres, 1857. vol. 65

índex

187

For information on additional titles,
write:

SUN CHALICE BOOKS
PO Box 9703
Albuquerque, New Mexico
USA 87119